Kiribati Island Travel and Tourism

People, Culture and Tradition, Environment

Author
David Saunders

Copyright Notice

Copyright © 2017 Global Print Digital
All Rights Reserved

Digital Management Copyright Notice. This Title is not in public domain, it is copyrighted to the original author, and being published by **Global Print Digital**. No other means of reproducing this title is accepted, and none of its content is editable, neither right to commercialize it is accepted, except with the consent of the author or authorized distributor. You must purchase this Title from a vendor who's right is given to sell it, other sources of purchase are not accepted, and accountable for an action against. We are happy that you understood, and being guided by these terms as you proceed. Thank you

First Printing: 2017.

ISBN: 978-1-912483-06-8

Publisher: Global Print Digital.
Arlington Row, Bibury, Cirencester GL7 5ND
Gloucester
United Kingdom.
Website: www.homeworkoffer.com

Table of Content

Introduction 1
  Land.. 2
Food and Economy 4
Politics... 9
  Government.. 9
The People, Cultural and Identity 12
  People.. 12
    Gender Roles and Statuses... 13
    Marriage, Family, and Kinship 13
    Socialization.. 14
    Medicine and Health Care 16
  Culture... 16
    Food, Dining and Drink 19
    Ethnicity, Language, & Religion 26
    Relationships, Marriage, & Family Life 29
    Social Life in Kiribati.. 30
    Traditional Clothing, songs, and dances 32
    Environment 34
    Art... 75
      Architecture of Kiribati 75
History 77
  In More Detail 82
Tourism 90
  Travel Guide 90
  Attractions.. 92
  Food and Restaurants 95
  Shopping and Leisure 97
  Transportation 98
  Things to do 100
    Wildlife 106
    Bird Watching in Kiribati.. 108
    Diving & Snorkeling 109
    Fishing... 111
    Surfing in Kiribati 115
    Kiribati Island Tours 117
    World War II Sight 119
    Islands... 121
      Kiritimati Island 121

  Tabiteuea Island 122
  Tarawa Island 124
Airports *127*
Travel Tips *128*
Visas and Vaccinations *130*
Holidays and Festivals *132*
Weather *134*

Introduction

Kiribati (pronounced "KIRR-i-bas") consists of three island groups in Polynesia and Micronesia, all of which are coral reefs, plus one volcanic island, the island of Banaba. Banaba is, like the coral reefs, not that high as the country's highest point, which is on that island, is only 260 feet (80 meters) above sea level.

In the far western part of the country is the island of Banaba, but also in the western part of the country are the 17 Gilbert Islands, all of which are in Micronesia. In the central part of the country are the 8 islands in the Phoenix Island Chain and in the east are the 8 islands in the Line chain, which sit wholly in Polynesia. All of these islands are coral reefs and most of them are bare as the soil is poor and there are almost no plants or trees anywhere on the islands outside of Banaba.

The ocean currents around Kiribati move from the east to the west and in the southern part of the country the currents shift to the south. Most of the people are actually Micronesian in origin (despite the country being geographically in Polynesia) and most of these early people arrived via the water with the ocean currents. However, these ocean currents aren't enough to attract regular visitors so over time the people on Kiribati became almost completely isolated and developed a unique culture.

Land

A few of the islands are compact with fringing reefs, but most are atolls. The largest atoll (and one of the largest in the world) is Kiritimati (Christmas) Atoll in the Line group, which has a land area of 150 square miles (388 square km) and accounts for almost half of the country's total area. Kiritimati was used for U.S. and British nuclear weapons testing in the 1960s; it now has a large coconut plantation and fish farms as well as several satellite telemetry stations. Banaba reaches 285 feet (87 metres) above sea level, the highest point in Kiribati. Its rich layer of phosphate was exhausted by mining from 1900 to 1979, and it is now sparsely inhabited. The rest of the atolls rise no higher than some 26 feet (8 metres), making them vulnerable to changes in ocean surface levels. By 1999 two unpopulated islets had been covered by the sea; the threat of rising sea levels, a theoretical result of global warming, would be disastrous for the islands of Kiribati. Average precipitation in the Gilbert group ranges from 120 inches (3,000 mm) in the north to 40 inches (1,000 mm) in the south, though all of the islands experience periodic droughts. Most rain falls in the season of westerly winds, from November through March; from April to October, northeast trade winds prevail. Temperatures are usually in the range of 80 to 90 °F (27 to 32 °C).

Coconut palms dominate the landscape on each island. Together with the products of the reef and the ocean, coconuts are the major contributors to village diet not only the nuts themselves but also the sap. The gathered sap, or toddy, is used in cooking and as a sweet beverage; fermented, it becomes an intoxicating drink. Breadfruit and pandanus also are grown. Cyrtosperma chamissonis, a coarse tarolike plant, can be cultivated in pits, but plants such as taro, bananas, and sweet potatoes are scarce. Pigs and chickens are raised.

Food and Economy

Food in Daily Life. Fish and marine resources are a primary food source, as the ecological nature of atolls mean that only the most hardy plants can grow there. Local crops include coconut, giant swamp taro, breadfruit, pandanus, and a native fig. Coconut is central to the diet and is especially valued for the sweet, vitamin-rich toddy (sap) cut from the flower spathe. Toddy is used as a children's drink or as a base for syrup. It can also be soured into vinegar and fermented into an alcoholic drink. Drunkenness is a widespread problem that is dealt with on some islands by the prohibition of alcohol. Imported goods, especially rice, but also flour, canned butter, and canned fish and meat, are becoming increasingly important in the daily diet.

Food Customs at Ceremonial Occasions. The display and eating of prestige foods is central to all celebrations and banquets. Although imported goods are increasingly available, local foods are more important in feasting, such as crayfish, giant clam, pig, chicken, and giant swamp taro. The most symbolically valued crop is giant swamp taro, which is grown in pits dug into the water lens under each atoll.

Basic Economy. Around 80 percent of the population engages in subsistence agriculture and fishing. The cash economy is limited largely to South Tarawa, where the private sector of the economy is very small and there are few manufacturing enterprises. Independence in 1979 coincided with the end of phosphate mining on Banaba, which in 1978 had accounted for 88 percent of the nation's export earnings. The cash economy has now shifted to dependence on remittances from I-Kiribati employed in phosphate mining on Nauru or working as seamen on foreign-owned merchant ships, as well as foreign aid. Accounting for some 60 percent of the gross domestic product in 1995, aid is received mainly from Japan, Australia, New Zealand, South Korea, and the European Union. The government has determined that there is potential for the development of tourism. However, economic development is constrained by a shortage of skilled workers, weak infrastructure, and geographic remoteness.

Land Tenure and Property. Access to and ownership of land underlie and cement social relations. A vital unit in I-Kiribati society, the *utu* includes all those people who are linked as kin and share common ownership of land plots. Everyone on an island belongs to several utu; people may inherit the land rights for each utu from either parent. The *kainga*, or family estate, sits at the heart of each utu, and those who live on the particular kainga of one of their utu have the greatest say in utu affairs and the largest share of produce from the land in that utu. The colonial government attempted to reorganize the land tenure system to encourage the codification of individual land holdings, in part to reduce land disputes. As a result, land transfers are now registered.

Commercial Activities. Marine resources have emerged as the most important natural resource for Kiribati, particularly the licensing of foreign fishing vessels to fish in the two hundred nautical miles of the exclusive economic zone in the waters surrounding the islands. Efforts to develop a competitive local fishing company have been less successful but large stocks of tuna fish remain in Kiribati waters. Copra, fish, and farmed seaweed are major exports.

Trade. The primary imports are food, manufactured goods, vehicles, fuel, and machinery. Most consumer goods are imported from Australia, and the Australian dollar is the unit of currency.

Until 1979, when Banaba's deposit of phosphate rock was exhausted, Kiribati's economy depended heavily on the export of that mineral. Before the cessation of mining, a large reserve fund was accumulated; the interest now contributes to government revenue. Other revenue earners are copra, mostly produced in the village economy, and license fees from foreign fishing fleets, including a special tuna-fishing agreement with the European Union. Commercial seaweed farming has become an important economic activity.

An Exclusive Economic Zone of 1,350,000 square miles (3,500,000 square km) is claimed. A small manufacturing sector produces clothing, furniture, and beverages for domestic consumption and sea salt for export. The country's proximity to the Equator makes it a desirable location for satellite telemetry and spacecraft-launching facilities; several national and transnational space authorities have built or have proposed building facilities on the islands or in surrounding waters.

Such projects bring capital, additional employment, and infrastructure improvements, but Kiribati continues to depend on foreign aid for most capital and development expenditure. Food accounts for about one-third of all imports, most of which come from Australia, Japan, and Singapore; Japan and Thailand are the major export destinations. Although South Tarawa has an extensive wage economy, most of the people living on outer islands are subsistence farmers with small incomes from copra, fishing, or handicrafts. These are supplemented by remittances from relatives working elsewhere. Interisland shipping is provided by the government, and most islands are linked by a domestic air service. Tarawa and Kiritimati have major airports.

Politics

Government.

The boti, or clan, system, which according to oral tradition was imported from Samoa around 1400C.E., remained the central focus of social and political life in Tungaru until around 1870. By the time of the establishment of the British protectorate in 1892, the traditional boti system had largely been eradicated, replaced judicially and administratively by a central government station on each island. Another major change came when the colonial administration completely reorganized the land tenure system before the 1930s, taking households that had been dispersed as hamlets in the bush and lining them up in villages along a central thoroughfare. At that time, control over village and family activities started to move to the heads of families. In 1963, the British colonial government abolished the kingship (*uea*) system that was part of the traditional political structure of the northern islands. The council of elders (*unimane*) that historically included all the male senior family heads is now responsible for overseeing village and island affairs. Local government consists of statutory island councils with elected members and limited administrative and financial powers and government-appointed administrators.

The government consists of aManeaba ni Maungatabu, or parliament, which is unicameral. The Beretitenti, or president, is elected by popular vote every four years and is both head of government and chief of state. There is no tradition of formal political parties, although there are loosely structured political parties. There is universal suffrage at age 18.

Leadership and Political Officials. The council of elders in each community continues to be an effective local political force. The village household is the most important unit, and within it the most important person is the oldest male.

Social Problems and Control. The judicial branch of the government includes a court of appeals and a high court, as well as a magistrate's court on each inhabited island. The jurisdiction of the magistrates' courts is unlimited in land matters but limited in criminal and civil cases. There are small police forces on all the islands. Emerging substantial problems include embezzlement (often connected with the practice of bubuti, or requests by kin that cannot be refused), robbery, sexual coercion, and child and domestic abuse, often linked to alcohol use.

Military Activity. There is no standing army. Kiribati has shown some assertiveness in its foreign relations, for example, in the 1986 fishing rights treaty that was negotiated with the Soviet Union despite strong opposition from the United States.

Nongovernmental Organizations and Other Associations

Nongovernmental organizations (NGO) include the Catholic and Protestant women's organizations and the Scouting Association and Guiding Association. An NGO of traditional healers was recently formed. Australian, British, Japanese, and American volunteer organizations are active in Kiribati.

David Saunders

The People, Cultural and Identity

People

The people are Micronesian, and the vast majority speak Gilbertese (or I-Kiribati). English, which is the official language, is also widely spoken, especially on Tarawa. More than half of the population is Roman Catholic, and most of the rest is Kiribati Protestant (Congregational). There are small minorities of Mormon and Bahā'ī followers.

For many years the population of most islands has remained fairly static because of migration to the rapidly growing urban centres of South Tarawa, where more than two-fifths of the population lives. South Tarawa, including Betio, the port and commercial centre of Tarawa, has an extremely high population density. Most people live in single-story accommodations. The rural population of Kiribati lives in villages dominated by Western-style churches and large open-sided thatched meetinghouses. Houses of Western-style construction are seen on outer islands and are common on Tarawa.

Gender Roles and Statuses

Division of Labor by Gender. Labor is divided by gender, with men fishing and collecting toddy and doing heavy construction tasks, while women handle child care and cook and keep house; both genders cultivate crops. While women may fish and often collect shellfish in the lagoon, only men may collect toddy. There is a clear status ranking in each household, which is usually headed by the oldest male unless he is too elderly to be active. The control of domestic activities lies with a senior married woman.

The Relative Status of Women and Men. While Kiribati society is currently egalitarian, democratic, and respectful of human rights, in the traditional culture women occupy a subordinate role. Job opportunities for women are limited, and there is no

law against gender discrimination. Few women have served in key governmental or political positions. Women have started to play a more prominent role through women's associations

Marriage, Family, and Kinship

Marriage. Although historically polygamy was practiced, the marriage system is now monogamous. Arranged marriages remain common, especially in rural areas. "Love matches" and elopements have become more common and are tolerated by most families. Virginity tests of the bride remain valued despite criticism by churches. Marriage is almost universal, and divorce is unpopular and uncommon.

Domestic Unit. The household is commonly based on a single nuclear family and may include aging parents and adoptive kin. Patrilocal residence remains common in rural areas, with married women moving to live on the husband's kainga.

Kin Groups. The main kinship units are mwenga ("household"), utu ("related family"), and kainga. Membership in mwenga is determined by residence, in utu by kin relations, and in kainga by common property holding and descent from a common ancestor. Inheritance of property and kinship are traced through both the mother's and the father's families. Adoption is widely practiced, especially between close kin.

Socialization

Infant Care. In this pro-natal society, infants are showered with attention and care by both parents and by the extended family. In the first few months after a birth, the mother stays in the house with the baby, and breast-feeding on demand is standard until at least six months of age. Kiribati has one of the highest infant death rates in the world as a result of diarrheal disease and respiratory infection.

Child Rearing and Education. After infancy, care by siblings, especially sisters, is very common, even by siblings as young as eight years. Children are indulged until they are about four years old, after which they become subject to strict parental and kin authority reinforced by corporal punishment. Crying and emotional outbreaks are not tolerated, and a good child is obedient, helpful, and respectful. By age eight or nine, children are expected to start helping around the house.

Schooling is compulsory for children from age six. Approximately 20 percent of primary students go on to receive secondary education. Education is highly valued by parents as a means of increasing their children's wage-earning abilities.

Higher Education. Higher education is expanding and increasingly valued. Kiribati participates with eleven other Pacific Island countries in funding the University of the South Pacific with its main campus in

Suva, Fiji. Technical education is available in South Tarawa at the Teacher's Training College, Tarawa Technical Institute, and the Marine Training Centre.

Medicine and Health Care

Life expectancy is low, and the most common causes of adult death are infectious diseases, including tuberculosis. Liver cancer is a common cause of male death, exacerbated by widespread infection with hepatitis B and heavy alcohol use. There have been several cases of AIDS. Traffic-related accidents are increasing.

While a new central hospital was completed in Tarawa in 1992 and the Ministry of Health and Family Planning provides free medical care in most villages, medical supplies and services are not always available. A pluralistic system of traditional herbal and massage treatments is maintained alongside biomedical services, and many women give birth at home. Healing traditions are passed on as special knowledge within families.

Culture

Kiribati (pronounced "KIRR-i-bas") consists of 33 atolls and a couple island chains making the country somewhat diverse, yet at the same time the people seem to live very similar lifestyles as cities are rare and life is approached slowly. Another thing that links the people is in their fight against global warming as rising water levels are sure to drown the country of Kiribati in the future as the country will disappear forever (many people are already moving to New Zealand).

Village life dominates in Kiribati and this life tends to revolve around the land, both in isolating the people on islands as well as providing food for the people in both plants and animals. Many people work the land to make a living and for these people this way of life seems to be at the core of the culture. Even the people living in the cities often have a lifestyle that revolves around the land as many occupations in Kiribati are dependent on the land and the sea. There are some service jobs and government jobs as well, most of which are found in the cities.

Most evenings are spent with family in the home, although some people also work at this time, especially those working the fields as the mid-day heat can be too much to handle so they work mornings and evenings. For some of these people the weekends are also occupied with work in order to feed their family or to maintain their standard of living. On weekends many young people enjoy getting together to play soccer (football), volleyball, or another sport. Also common for people of all ages are impromptu visits to see neighbors, family, or friends. These visits may only last a few minutes or hours. For larger celebrations the whole community may gather in the local *maneaba*, perhaps after church on Sunday.

Identity

The people of Kiribati tend to identify as either i-Kiribati or Gilbertese, which is an identity defined by a combination of country, language, religion, culture, and lifestyle. Nearly everyone in Kiribati identifies in this way and it is strongly attached to the culture and lifestyle of the people. This includes their religion, language, and lifestyle among others. This identity is somewhat attached to the political entity as well, but anyone from the country who lives outside is borders is also considered to be i-Kiribati or Gilbertese as well. It is important to note that this identity includes all people in Kiribati, not just those people in the "Gilbert Islands."

Kiribati society remains conservative and resistant to change; ties to family and traditional land remain strong, and conspicuous displays of individual achievement or wealth are discouraged. The building and racing of sailing canoes is a common pastime. Musical composition and dancing in customary styles are regarded as art forms and are the basis of widespread competition. Volleyball and football (soccer) are popular sports.

Food, Dining and Drink

Historic Diet

Most of the islands in Kiribati (pronounced "KIRR-i-bas") are coral reefs so there is little soil and a lack of plant life on most of the islands. Also with few plants there are few animals on the islands, although the surrounding seas are full of animals that the earliest inhabitants used for food, including crabs, turtles, fish of all kinds, and sea birds such as noddies and terns.

The most important plant used for food in Kiribati, both in the past and perhaps today, is the coconut, which made its way to the islands by water. The coconut is the staple food for the people in the past and this continues today as this food is used for its milk and flesh. The coconut is one of the only plants that made its way to Kiribati prior to the islands' first settlers, although these settlers later brought with them numerous plants and animals that make up much of today's diet.

Culinary Influences

When the first people arrived to the islands of Kiribati they brought with them foods in the form of plants and animals. Later waves of people also brought additional plants and animals. These plants and animals included pigs, rats, dogs, taro, rice, yams, breadfruit, bananas, lemons, and sugarcane among others. Although it's not known when or with whom many of these foods arrived, it is clear they arrived with the early waves of settlers and all were present by 1200 at the latest.

The next major outside influence on the diet likely began in the 900s when the Tongans took control over many islands in the South Pacific. They strongly influenced the people of Polynesia in terms of language, religion, and culture, so it's likely they also influenced the food, but it is unknown in what way. It is clear that Polynesian cuisine became quite uniform at some point and this may have happened in the 900-1400s as communication throughout all of Polynesia peaked, beginning under the influence of the Tongans.

Among the many culinary links throughout Polynesia, one of the most significant is a cooking method that begins with rocks that are heated then placed in the ground as they are topped with food wrapped in banana leaves and covered in dirt. This essentially acts as a pressure cooker and can be found throughout Polynesia. Although when it began is unknown, it is common in New Zealand among the

Maori so this cooking method likely existed prior to about 1300, which is about when the Maori settled that country from Polynesia.

Foreigners didn't make any settlement efforts until the 1800s, at which point they began to influence and change the food in Kiribati. These settlers, primarily British and Americans, brought their own foods to the islands as they introduced cattle, chickens, wheat, potatoes, cassava, watermelons, pineapples, papayas, oranges, mangoes, onions, and tomatoes among many others. These foods added to the local diet and gave these foreign settlers a familiar diet, but most locals still relied heavily on their historic diet.

Through the 1900s few significant culinary influences arrived to Kiribati, although better communication, transportation, and technology gave the people access to imported foods and non-perishable goods, hence extending the shelf life of many foods. Today these foods make an impact on the diet as canned meats are common and western foods and restaurants are arising in some areas, particularly those islands catering to the tourists. However, the locals tend to maintain their historic diets with the addition of these imported foods.

When & Where to Eat

Most people in Kiribati start the day with a small breakfast. This may be fruit, breads, coffee, tea, or the previous day's leftovers. No matter the food it tends to be small and eaten at home.

Lunch was always the largest and longest meal of the day in Kiribati as people would return home to eat a large meal and perhaps take a nap afterwards to avoid the hottest part of the day outside. This is still common in many villages, especially among farmers, fishers, and others who spend their time outside. In most places lunch has become a shorter meal as most people eat at work or school.

For these workers that eat lunch at work, dinner is the largest meal of the day now and it tends to be a large feast with the family. Often times there is enough food made for this meal and the following day's breakfast and lunch. For those people who have a large lunch, dinner tends to be a bit smaller and usually consists of the leftovers from lunch.

Staple Foods

Breadfruit (*ulu*): this fruit is very common
Coconut: coconuts are used for their milk and flesh
Pandanus: this fruit is common on some islands and is often boiled before being eaten
Rice: a common base or side for many meals

Taro: taro root is prepared in numerous ways, including as *poi*; it is one of the main staples throughout Polynesia

Yams: yams, a member of the potato family, are found in many meals

Regional Variations, Specialties, & Unique Dishes

Palu sami: coconut cream, onion, and curry powder wrapped in taro leaves; often served with pork or chicken

Dining Etiquette

Dining in Kiribati varies a bit depending on the setting and your company. Generally, the dining in Kiribati is less formal than it is in many countries and rules are more relaxed. Despite this, there are some formal restaurants in the country and if dining in a business setting rules are more important.

The formalities and most important aspects of dining in Kiribati are related to behavior more than actual eating. For example, bringing food to a dinner, even a small side dish or dessert can be a great offense to the host by indicating they will not prepare enough food for everyone. Also let your host seat you as guests are also often asked to sit in the middle of the table so they may converse with everyone more easily.

Once seated, and you must be sitting to eat, you may notice silverware (cutlery) or it may be absent. Many of the people eat with their hands and if this is the case do the same, although they may offer a fork or spoon. If you do eat with your hands a bowl of water will likely be passed around before (and after) the meal to wash your hands. Prior to taking your food be aware that taking a second serving is rude so take everything you plan to eat before eating (even if this plate is huge as many of the locals will do) and be sure to try every dish offered as this is a sign of appreciation and respect.

Don't begin eating until indicated to do so; your host may expect you to start eating first as the guest, but don't assume this. Most meals also begin with a blessing of some sort and you shouldn't start eating until this. Try to eat at the same pace as everyone else so everyone begins and finishes eating at about the same time. Most of the people will leave some food behind then will take their excess food home for a latter meal. You are welcome to do the same, but as a guest your host may insist you finish your food.

If dining in a restaurant, many of the above rules also apply, but there will most definitely be eating utensils and the setting will be more formal (although it will still be less formal than most of Europe, Australia, or North America). The host of a meal is expected to pay for everyone present; if this is you check for a service charge on the bill. Often times a 10% service charge is included in the bill so no additional tip is needed. If there is no service charge on the bill, tip at your discretion.

Drinks

Today nearly any popular international beverage can be found in Kiribati, such as juices, soft drinks, tea, and coffee. However for a more authentic taste of the South Pacific try *kava*. This drink is made from the kava plant's roots, which are ground to release liquid, then water is added and the juice is drunk. This drink gives a very relaxing effect, yet is not considered a drug in the countries of the South Pacific.

Beer is overwhelmingly the most popular alcoholic beverage in Kiribati among the locals, but there are no local breweries so all beer is imported. Hard liquors and wine are also typically available in hotels and nice restaurants, but the selection is somewhat limited in most locations.

The tap water is not safe to drink in Kiribati; in fact in many areas you shouldn't even swim in it due to small organisms that can penetrate your skin. You should entirely avoid the tap water and items that could be made from or with the water, such as ice, fruits, and salads.

Ethnicity, Language, & Religion

Ethnicity

Almost everyone in Kiribati is ethnically Micronesian. The Micronesians are a combination of Melanesian, Polynesian, and Filipino, but each group of Micronesians is quite distinct from the next as some tend to be more Filipino in ethnicity, language, food, and culture while others have more pronounced Polynesian attributes, which is the case with the people of Kiribati. It seems the first settlers were Austronesian, but later waves of people arrived and intermarried, including those from Melanesia and Polynesia, over time creating the ethnic group that exists today. Perhaps the closest relatives to the i-Kiribati are the Marshallese and other Micronesian people, but with a more distant relation to the Samoansand Tongans.

Language

All throughout the inhabited Gilbert and Line islands, the people communicate with one another with our mother tongue, the Kiribati language. The English language however became our official language as well. Today both languages are spoken and used interchangeably for official purposes and on a daily basis.

Gilbertese or Kiribati (or sometimes Kiribatese) is a language from the Austronesian family, part of the Oceanian branch and of the Nuclear Micronesian subbranch. It has a basic verb–object–subject word order.

The word *Kiribati* is just the modern rendition for "Gilberts", so the name is not usually translated into English. "Gilberts" comes from Captain Thomas Gilbert, who, along with Captain John Marshall, was one of the first Europeans to discover the Gilbert Islands in 1788. The official name of the language is *te taetae ni Kiribati*, or 'the Kiribati language'.

The first complete description of this language was in *Dictionnaire gilbertin–français* of Father Ernest Sabatier (981p, 1954), a Catholic priest. This Dictionary was later translated into English by Sister Olivia (with the help of South Pacific Commission).

About 105,000 people speak Gilbertese, 98,000 of whom live in Kiribati, about 97.2% of the entire population. The others are the inhabitants of Nui (Tuvalu), Rabi Island (Fiji), Mili (Marshall Islands) and some other islands where I-Kiribati have been relocated

(Solomon Islands, notably Choiseul Province, and Vanuatu) or emigrated (to New Zealand and Hawaii mainly).

Unlike many in the Pacific region, the Kiribati language is far from extinct, and most speakers use it daily. Only 30% of Kiribati speakers are fully bilingual with English.

Fishermen, sailors, farmers and people involved in the production of copra comprise the majority of Kiribati speakers.

Religion
Religious Beliefs. The forerunners of the present-day Kiribati Protestant Church (K.P.C.), the American Board of Commissioners for Foreign Missions and the London Missionary Society, arrived in the northern and southern islands, respectively, in 1857 and 1870. The French Roman Catholic fathers of the Order of the Sacred Heart began work on Nonouti in 1888. Catholics (53 percent of the indigenous population) are in the majority from Tarawa northward. The K.P.C. (41 percent) holds a near-monopoly on Arorae and Tamana and retains majorities on a few of the other southern islands. About 2½ percent of the I-Kiribati adhere to the Baha'i faith. Mormons, Seventh-Day Adventists, and members of other Christian sects make up the remainder of the population. A good deal of

social, recreational, and even economic activity centers on the churches.

Religious Practitioners. The expatriate (mostly French) Catholic clergy has been largely replaced by I-Kiribati priests and nuns. Local catechists conduct services on most islands between occasional visits by a priest. K.P.C. ministers are all I-Kiribati (except for a few from Tuvalu) but do not serve on their home islands. The priests of the old pagan religion interpreted omens and made offerings to deities that descended from time to time onto pillars of coral limestone and other shrines or took animal forms. Spirit mediums are probably still active, although they are possessed by recently introduced supernaturals and are regarded with great ambivalence. I-Kiribati deities (some with western Polynesian names) were believed to have been ancestors of descent groups that obeyed their taboos and relied on them for protection. Their associations with animals and natural phenomena gave them significance for the community as a whole.

Relationships, Marriage, & Family Life

Dating in Kiribati varies to a great degree as some young people today are able to date and choose their spouse, but for others dating is non-existent as families choose their children's spouse. Although this arranged marriage was much more common in the past, it still exists to some degree in Kiribati today.

Young, unmarried women are expected to maintain their virginity prior to marriage and if they do the wedding is a great celebration. However, if this is not the case the wedding ceremony will often take place in rather humble circumstances like at a courthouse or without a large celebration. This is because a significant part of the wedding night is proving that the girl was a virgin, in what is known as the "cloth ceremony," which demands that after the couple consummate their marriage they reveal the blood-stained sheet. If the bride isn't a virgin the families are often ashamed and a marriage can be immediately ended. In some cases however, if the bride loses her virginity to her groom then a staged "cloth ceremony" may take place.

After a couple is married, the bride's family will often travel with the cloth to extended family and the newly married couple will start a family of their own. Families in Kiribati vary in size, but most married women have three children, although some families are smaller and others are obviously larger.

Social Life in Kiribati

Behavior
The people of Kiribati are very humble and modest as they rarely express themselves in a way to offend another. This comes in respecting other people, dressing modestly, avoiding outward signs of wealth or affection, and having a reverence for God as most people are Christian.

As a visitor to Kiribati, that same modesty is expected; modesty in dress, actions, words, and every aspect of your life. Many of the most important behavioral restrictions to be aware of are related to dress, dating (see above for both), and dining (see our Kiribati Food & Dining Page for more information). Also try to avoid being loud, rude, showing off wealth, or getting drunk in public.

Dress
Historically the people of Kiribati wore very little clothing and today this has only slightly changed. In the past the people likely wore simple loin cloths for men and grass skirts for women, but today western-styled clothing dominates the country. Men generally wear shorts and light shirts or t-shirts while women often wear loose fitting light dresses.

As a visitor to Kiribati you may wear nearly anything, but nudity on beaches and elsewhere is considered inappropriate. In fact, any swimwear should be kept to beaches and private resorts. Outside these beaches shorts or skirts, preferably those that reach below the knee, as well as short-sleeved shirts are perfectly acceptable. Some people may prefer to wear long-sleeved shirts and pants along with a sun hat just to protect themselves from the sun.

Traditional Clothing, songs, and dances

Primitively and long ago the Kiribati people cover their bodies with dry woven coconut leaves both for men and women. These later became our specially made dance costumes in which we dance a variety of local dances in. Nowadays, imported sheets of material with different colors are sewn into what we call a lavalava.

It is worn mostly by everyone; men and women, the young and the old. For the ladies; a skillfully-made top named te Tiibuta is worn together with the lavalava. The boys can just wear the lavalava alone. Depending on each person's taste in fashion, the lavalava is sometimes embroidered and for men, they usually wear it short just above the knees.

The music of Kiribati has been less affected by Western culture than most other Pacific island cultures since Europeans did not arrive in Kiribati until 1892. The national anthemof Kiribati is "Teirake kaini

Kiribati" (*Stand Kiribati*), by Urium Tamuera Ioteba; it was adopted upon independence in 1979.

Kiribati folk music is generally based around chanting or other forms of vocalizing, accompanied by body percussion. Public performances in modern Kiribati are generally performed by a seated chorus, accompanied by a guitar. However, during formal performances of the standing dance (*Te Kaimatoa*) or the hip dance (*Te Buki*) a wooden box is used as a percussion instrument. This box is constructed so as to give a hollow and reverberating tone when struck simultaneously by a chorus of men sitting around it. Traditional songs are often love-themed, but there are also competitive, religious, children's, patriotic, war and wedding songs. There are also stick dances (which accompany legends and semi-historical stories. These stick dances or 'tirere' (pronounced seerere) are only performed during major festivals.

Folk song composition
Its traditional music is composed by people known as *te kainikamaen*. These composers are said to receive their songs from myth or magic, an ability that is said to pass from father to son. After composition, a group called *rurubene* sings the song to the composer, after which it is made public and is sung by anyone; at this point, the song is considered blessed (*mamiraki*).

Composers also write songs on demand, telling a story told to him by an individual. The composer will then sing it and teach it to the *rurubene*, making any needed changes. Composers also occasionally create songs of their own accord.

Environment

There was often a shortage of water in the southern Gilberts (Kiribati) - especially towards the end of the dry season. About October, Butaritari atoll in the north had a more conventional tropical climate, with 100-120 in. of rain a year, and Tarawa (the capital of the Republic of Kiribati), could usually count on 60-70 in., but at the southern end of the group, the average was less than 50 in.; on Beru atoll, it was 45 in., almost all of it between November and March.

From May to September the main sources of fresh water, apart from a few brackish wells, were squalls which from time to time came stalking over the eastern horizon, trailing great curtains of rain. When a squall was seen approaching, the islanders had other preoccupations. There was always great excitement - due partly to a natural awe (for the Gilbertese (I-Kiribati) a rain cloud, like everything else, had a life and purpose of its own), partly to speculation about which end of the lagoon it would cross and whether there was time to reach it before the rain passed. There would be a rush to load canoes with nuts, gourds, tins, clam shells and old sails to catch water in. Often a whole village would set off down the lagoon to intercept a squall, and then sail with it out to sea for as long as they could keep up. In the fastest canoes this might be for half an hour or more, and afterwards a long beat home against the Trades with their 'catch', when inevitably some would be spilled and some would be spoiled, but always a little would be saved to give some meaning to the day's endeavour. The Gilbertese rainclouds, though awesome, were nevertheless benign: they were messengers of the Gods, sent to catch up the souls of dying people and carry them to Paradise:

If a small sudden shower of rain came over a village, it was believed that a soul had just passed. The shower was called *wa-n-te-mate*, the canoe of the dead. If such a shower came when a man lay dying, and passed on leaving him still alive, the people beside him would say to each other, '*Ai Kawa-ra ngke e aki oa wa-na*' (How unfortunate when he not catch his canoe). And if another cloud was expected to arrive soon, the sick man would be encouraged to release his ghost quickly, so that it might pass easily with the rain.

A concrete example of this happened in Tarawa, the capital of Kiribati, early in 1916, just after the completion of the gruesome office of hanging a murderer. As the people quitted the gallows chamber, a tiny shower passed over the building. One of the native officials, who had been particularly depressed by the distressing business, immediately recovered his spirits and said cheerfully, '*Akea te bai iai, ba e bon roko-raoi wa-na*'. (It's quite all-right, for it certainly arrives-well his canoe).

The art of bonesetting as practised by the Gilbertese is free from magic or ritual of any kind. The splints used for broken bones are made of coconut slithers and the strong outer skin of the *babai* stalk. Bandages are of *babai* bark cut to the same length as the splints. For injuries to the trunk a bed is made of the spathes of coconut blossom, stripped and flattened.

Diagnosis: If there is a burning sensation in the skin over the fracture, it is a pain caused by the flesh and the blood. If you feel an itching and smarting pain, it is caused by flesh and vein. If you feel *maraki ae waewaerake* (aching and throbbing) it is pain of bone and flesh. Before applying a splint the blood is always driven towards the fracture by three massages a day - just after sunrise, at noon and just before sunset. for complicated fractures, massage is applied about every two hours for the first three days, three times on the fourth day and after. For longstanding disability caused by an old imperfectly mended fracture, the patient is taken out into the lagoon and massaged there, floating in warm sea water. Gentle pressure is applied, sometimes for many weeks, to straighten the limb. The patient is taught to walk first in the sea and then gradually on shore. Splints are bound on to a fracture for three days. some fractures like splints, others do not. If a fracture is uncomfortable in splints you hold the fracture in place and press gently on the part which is painful. The splints are intended not so much to support the fractured bone as to relieve pain. At your first visit to a man with a fractured bone, you massage his stomach. The following is the usual timetable, regulated by the sun:

At sunrise: Massage of *te iriko* (flesh), *te rara* (blood), *te ia* (veins).

About 9 a.m.: Gentle rubbing along the limb, from each side in towards the fracture (*te torotorobi*).

At noon: *Te tai ni kaokiri* (the time to put back the bone). All the manipulation of the fractured bone is made at this hour.

About 3 p.m.: *Te torotorobi* again.

At sunset: Massage of flesh, blood and veins.

About 9 p.m.: Massage of flesh, blood and veins.

At midnight: Manipulation of bone.

About 3 a.m.: Massage of flesh, blood and veins.

This treatment lasts for three days. After the third day the healer visits at sunrise, noon, sunset and midnight, working on the bone at noon and midnight only, massaging at the other hours. On rainy days no massage is performed, in case of pain on those days, the healer exerts gentle pressure on the injured part to reduce the pain.

If the patient has had no motion for three days since injury, he is given a copious drink of boiled coconut toddy very hot with water. If constipation continues he is given molasses with hot water and cream of coconut flesh.

A cure for Riki-ni-biroto (*distended stomach i.e. dyspepsia*) from *Nui, Ellice Islands (now Tuvalu)*. Choose a *kiaou (triumfetta procumbena)* creeper that grows a short distance from the house; it must have three branches. Then go back to your house and draw a deep breath: run without breathing to the *kiaou* and pluck one of its branches. Hold this in the right hand and, still without breathing, run three times round the plant. You may then draw breath again and walk slowly back to the house with the branch you have picked.

Pick a nut in the *moi* stage, before it has fallen from the tree. Grate the flesh and mix the gratings with the curd-like substance contained in the *moi*. Put the mixture into a *kumete* (wooden bowl) and pound it up with the stalk, leaves, flowers and seeds of the *kiaou* plant, until it makes a soft mach. Turn the mash out upon a piece of the fibrous material that grows at the base of the coconut leaf; wrap it up in this and wring it dry of juice into a coconut shell. Boil the juice in its shell, and let the patient drink it as hot as possible.

Drought for an expectant mother, who thinks that her child is moving too much in the uterus or that a fall or blow may have injured it. Ingrediest: Take one nut in the *moi* stage and two in the *ura* stage. (Te moi is the freshly fallen nut. At the *ura* stage the nut is ripe, and its flesh is brown throughout). Grate their flesh and mix it. Wring out the gratings in the fibrous 'cloth' of the coconut and allow the cream to drip into a wooden bowl. Heat the cream over a fire in half a coconut shell. Skim off and throw away the frothy scum which arises. After more heating, the coconut-oil appears. Remove from the fire at the point and mix with an equal quantity of water. The mixture is then re-heated and given to the patient to drink. Immediately afterwards, she must drink the water of as many coconuts as she can manage, and then eat their flesh.

Next day the physician gathers from the bush one handful each of tips of young *kanawa* shoots (*cordia subcordata*); flowers of the *bingibing* (*thespesia procumbena*). These are first pounded together and then 'wrung' of their juice into the water of five drinking coconuts. The mixture is given to the patient, to be finished at a single sitting. The treatment continues if necessary.

Feverishness (te kabuoki-te-mariri--*the-burning-the-cold)*. All sweet-smelling trees are considered good by native practitioners, i.e. any part of a tree may be used for fever-medicine if it produces a sweet-smelling flower or leaf. The auri (*ghettardo speciosa*) and the *ango* (*premna taitensis*) are chiefly favoured, while the kianga-ni-makin (*polypodium*) and *kaura* (*wedelia stringulosaa*) are used when procurable. The bark, roots, flowers and tips of young branches are gathered, a handful of each. These are chopped up fine and boiled in a giant clam-shell with well water, one coconut shell full for each handful of ingredients. When it is cold, the patient both drinks it and washes his body with it.

Piecing the ears. The earlobes of a boy or girl are not pierced until the subject is twelve to fourteen years old. The operator is normally a member of the family, but this is not essential. The instrument used is a skewer-like piece of wood, called *Kangeri* (make-curl) because it is also used for teasing the hair into curls. It is generally made of pemphis-wood and so can be sharpened to a very fine, hard point. Each morning is the time for the operation. The operator sits facing the subject; as a pad to support the lobe of the ear, he uses the half of a *nimoimoi*, a very young coconut, just developed, and not more than an inch in diameter. He begins on the right ear. Holding he 'pad' in his left hand, he inserts it behind the lobe so that the latter lies on its flat surface and is turned towards him. Then he pierces the flesh with the *kangeri*. Immediately withdrawing the instrument, he introduces a stalk of smooth grass into the puncture, and leaves it there. The same process is repeated on the left ear, the pad being held now in the right hand of the operator.

In the evening, the stalks of grass are removed, hot water being used to soften the clotted blood. When the grass has been taken out, it is replaced by slightly thicker stalks. On the following morning, exactly the same thing happens; and so on, morning and evening every day, the grass being thickened at each sitting. When the largest size of grass has been reached, the stalks of the leaves of the *bingbing* in ascending thickness are inserted; and when the limit of these is arrived at, young *babai* stalks are employed. This process gradually distends the lobe until in about three weeks' time the aperture will accept a stalk about as thick as the thumb. This is the size generally recognized as the normal standard by the Gilbertese.

By now the lobes of the patient's ears are probably sore and festering; healing methods are therefore used. Leaves of the *mao* are picked and their midribs removed; they are then rolled into cylinders of the requisite size, i.e. a thumb's thickness, heated at the fire and inserted in the apertures. Fomentations of hot water are continued morning and evening, when new rolls of *mao*leaf are inserted. When the outside edges of the wounds become clean, but still a little rawness remains within the ring, the cylinders of mao leaf are replaced by rolls of *manibwebwe*, which is he glossy sun-dried skin taken from the underside of a pandanus leaf. A week or so after this the ear will be healed. Those who wish to leave larger apertures can proceed from this point, further distension being effected by inserting articles of increasing size. The limit of size is normally considered to have been reached when the loop of the lobe can just be taken over the top of the ear. In this way it is carried when not in use.

No magico-religious rituals or beliefs appear to be connected with the piercing of earlobes. The old men of today, most of whom have this personal adornment, consider it simply as a practical means of beautifying the person. Any object which appeals to the aesthetic taste of the individual may be more in the aperture. On Butaritari (in 1933) an old man carrying in one lobe his pipe and in another a small red fish. Most generally seen as ear ornaments among the older people are rolls of golden-yellow pandanus leaf burnished with scented oil, and the sweet-smelling sheath of the pandanus bloom Rosettes and ornaments made of the pith (*uto*) of the scaevola shrub were commonly used in the past.

Poisons

(a) Used in fishing

For stupefying fish in pools on the reef, the seed of a tree called *baireati* is used in the northern islands. One or two *baireati* trees grow in Butaritari and Little Makin, but the supply of seed is mainly obtained from the western beach of any island, where it is sometimes washed ashore in considerable numbers during the season of westerly gales. Its thick envelope of husk renders it capable of travelling great distances oversea. The *baireati* is conjecturally identified as *Barringtonia butonica*. The seed is taken out of the husk and grated on a rasp of cured sting-ray skin; the gratings are then scattered in the pool as desired. A very small quantity suffices to poison a large sheet of water; on a calm day, fragments allowed to sink into five-fathom water off the edge of a reef will stupefy fish in the near neighbourhood.

Another stupefying agent used in both the north and the south is the *ntabanin*, a small thin variety of sea-slug. The creature is taken alive and shredded on a grater, and the fragments are thrown into the water of a pool, where their effect is almost immediate. Some of the fish float in a comatose condition to the surface, others continue to swim lethargically below water; it is noticeable that the latter become quite blind, making no attempt to avoid any rocks that may stand in their way, or to escape the hand of the fisher. Fish stupefied with *te baireati* or *te ntabanin* are eaten with no further precaution than gutting before being cooked.

(b) For homicidal purposes

Neither of these poisons appears ever to have been used against human beings, their respective smells being considered to convey too clear a warning of their presence; the Gilbert Islander uses that sensitive organ, his nose, to an extent undreamed of by Europeans. The *buni*, or trigger-fish (*Tetradon*), formerly provided the most effective human poison known to the Gilbertese (I-Kiribati). The flesh of the *buni* may be eaten with perfect safety (in these waters) if the gall-sac (*ari*), liver (*ato*), alimentary canals (*ninika*) and roe (*bia*) be first removed without rupture, but these parts, and above all the gall-sac, contain a virulent poison, which is swiftly absorbed by the flesh if rupture takes place before the fish be gutted. The usual trick of the native poisoner apparently was to spill the contents of the gall-sac into the abdominal cavity during the removal of the viscera. This was sufficient to secure the death of any who ate the flesh.

The symptoms of *buni*-poisoning are well known to the modern race, as accidental cases still occur from time to time. The sense of balance is first affected, the knees give way, the legs become paralysed and death quickly supervenes. The poison appears to be of a neurotoxic order. The native treatment is to administer copious draughts of sea-water as soon as possible, in order to induce vomiting.

Te bwatua, a little teleost fish of the order *Plectognathi,* probably the small fry of one of the globe-fish, was also used by the poisoner of old days, the viscera being ruptured and inserted into the abdominal cavity of any other fish being cooked for food-purposes. As described by an old man of Marakei, the symptoms produced in the victim seem to have been similar to those of *buni*-poisoning.

Te kaweana, a crab with a light carapace and very long legs was known and used on Banaba and in the Northern Gilberts. All parts of this creature are said to be poisonous. The meat was shredded and cooked inside the food intended for the victim. The symptoms are described as 'sleepiness, heaviness of the senses *(te aawa)* increasing quickly to extreme lethargy, and final unconsciousness followed by death'. No pain appears to have been caused by the poison.

A horrible method of killing was used in Butaritari, Little Makin, Marakei and perhaps other islands. A great number of cantharides beetles were first collected by the poisoner and 'wrung out' in a piece of *ing* (the fibrous material at the base of the coconut-leaf); the juice thus obtained was mixed with *kamaimai,* and the drink offered to the victim. The fluid secreted by the cantharides beetle being a powerful vesicatory, causes inflammation throughout the *uro*-genital tract. In some cases acute membraneous cystitis may occur, as many Europeans know to their cost after having drunk coconut-toddy into which a few cantharides beetles have accidentally fallen. The victim of a draught containing the juice of some hundreds of these creatures must have died a terrible, lingering death.

A poison rarely used, because seldom obtainable at the right moment, was the liver of a shark. Under normal conditions, this is perfectly safe food, but individuals of the blue-shark species are said by natives to have a liver of aberrant shape, one lobe of which is recurved like a hook; in this condition it is stated to be very poisonous. The symptoms are those of neurotoxaemia.

Ancestor Cult
Stone columns
All through the Gilberts, stone monoliths *(boua)* ranging from eighteen inches in height were erected to the various spiritual 'powers'. Generally thee powers were considered to be gods, and they were the gods of the fair-skinned race, for their names were Taburimai, Auriaria, Tituaabine and so on. On Bairiki, an islet of Tarawa, there was a stone which was considered to be the '*rabata*' of the goddess Tituabine. This deity was the '*atua*' (family ghost) of the Bairiki family group, which treated her as a guardian spirit, abstained from eating the flesh of her creature, the Stingray, and made offerings of coconuts and food at full-moon every month to her stone.

The stone was set in a small square of broken coral slabs. Beside it were strews the bones and skulls of other ancestors in the Bairiki family group. In October 1922 they included the following:

7 Skulls	56 Ribs
5 Scapulae	12 Phalanges
1 Atlas	1 Inferior Maxillary
5 Humeri	2 Superior Maxillaries
5 Radii	22 Vertebrae
2 Ulnae	1 Femur
1 Sacrum	

These bones were anointed with oil when offerings were made to the stone around which they lay. The necessity to pay them reverence and to make offerings of food to them was recognized to be as pressing as the need to offer at Tituaabine's *'rabata'* (body - here it seems to be something between a shrine and an oracle) - the real men. Teitirere of Marakei, an old man of over eighty, described the cult of his ancestor Teweia. The *utu* (family group) descended from Teweia had a stone, about half a man's height, set up as a post in the ground on the east side of the island. This stone was called the body of Teweia: nevertheless, it was not considered to be the actual atua or spiritual power, which was the ghost of Teweia, but it was the medium through which the ghost was approached, and was so inalienably connected with the ghost, that whosoever did it an insult caused pain to the spiritual power, and was liable to sudden death or illness. On top of the monolith were perched three lumps of red coral: each was about as big as two fists. These were said to be the head of Teweia. A flat stone was laid on the ground at the western side of the base of the monolith. On this stone were laid all offerings of food brought to the ghost.

On occasions of stress or danger, the senior member of the *utu* would signify that a general assembly (*te toa*) would be made at the stone for the purpose of offering gifts of food to the ghost and *tataro* or prayers for his help. On the appointed day, the *utu* would rise at cock-crow and gather by the stone before sunrise, squatting in a semicircle on its west side and facing east towards it. They brought with them food, whose first portions - and later also sticks of tobacco and a filled pipe - were laid on the flat offering-stone. Then the *utu* would eat the remainder in silence. When the meal was done, the people put on their heads each a fillet made of a single pinnule from the crest of a coconut-tree, knotted in front. Then the senior male of the *utu* would squat before the stone and address to it, in his own words, the request which they had come to make. After this, the people dispersed, leaving the offerings on the stone of offering.

Also on Marakei was a stone bearing he name of Uaakeia, leader of the Beruan conquerors who had invaded and settled Marakei nine generations before. At this stone the *utu* descendants through the male and female line from Uaakeia made their *tataro* in time of need. The stone was broad and flat, being set in a recumbent position, not standing. Beneath it were buried the skulls of ancestors descended from Uaakeia, and also the skull of Uaakeia himself. Near the village of Temotu was a *boua* erected to Kaieti, another great fighter and voyager. In times of stress his descendants gathered to offer this prayer beside his stone at dawn:

Aora te amarake, Kaieti-o! Buoki-ra;

Our offering of food, Kaieti-o! Help us;

Tautau mauri-ra; toutoua nake te buaka;

Kee hold on our safety; tread away the war;

oro-ia, bakarere-ia itui matia;

strike them, pierce them, string their eyes together; *

ti aki bua ti aki taro; te mauri

we are not lost, we are not deserted; safety

ao te raoi, te mauri.

and peace; safety.

*As fish are strong together by the eyes to carry them home.

Tabakea the Ancestor

As a rule, each separate Gilbertese totem-group practised the cult of its own ancestral deities independently of all others; but in time of famine, a form of ritual meal in which all groups united, with the senior male of *Karongoa-n-uea* as the officiating priest, was practised at a stone pillar representing the body of a being named Tabakea, within a *maneaba* of particular style called Maunga-tabu. The being Tabake, upon whom the ritual to be described was centred, is associated with four totems: (1) A mythical beast called *te kekenu*, described as 'a lizard as big as two men' -no doubt a crocodile or alligator; (2) the common noddy; (3) a small tree called *te ibi,* which bears a scarlet almond-like fruit; (4) th3 turtle. Of these, the last is the most important, the name Tabakea itself meaning parrot-bill turtle. In a widespr4ead series of traditions Tabakea is represented as the Eldest of All Beings, the First of Things, and in all the tales which deal with the adventures and voyages of Auriaria, he appears as Auriaria's father. This doubtless explains why Auriaria's name is linked with Tabakea's in the formula which will presently be exhibited.

When famine threatened the community, the elder of *Karongoa-n-uea* would fix a day when food offerings and *tataro* (supplication) should be made to Tabakea; and a stone monolith six to nine feet high, representing the body of the god, would be erected for that purpose up against the Karongoa Sun-stone of the *maneaba*. The monolith was wreathed with coconut leaves by the acolyte group, *Karongoa-raereke*. Just before dawn on the appointed day, the community would enter the building, bringing with them offerings of food, and sit in their respective clan-places. Exactly at sunrise a watcher posted to observe the eastern horizon would call, '*E oti Taai (the sun appears)*' and a portion of food would be laid by the elder of the *Karongoa-n-uea* before the stone of the god, to the accompaniment of the following *tataro*:

Ao-ra te amarake, ngkoe, Tabakea.	*Our offering the food, thou, Tabakea.*
Ao-ra te amarake, ngkoe,	*Our offering the food, thou,*

Auriaria,	*Auriaria,*
Nei Tevenei, Riiki.	*Nei Tevenei, Riiki*
Tautaua mauri-ra, toutoua-nake te	*Uphold our prosperity, tread away*
rongo, te baki, te mate.	*the drought, the hunger, the death.*
Kakamauri-ia ataei aikai;	*Continue to prosper their children,*
Karerekea kara-ra.	*Continue to get our food.*
Taai-o, Namakaina-o!	*Sun-o, Moon-o!*
Karerekea kara-ra!	*Continue to get our food!*
Te mauri ma te raoi.	*Prosperity and peace.*

During this ceremony, all present, whether of the clan of Karongoa or not, wore the fillet of coconut leaf known as 'the fillet of the sun' (*buna-n taai*). The formula having been recited three times, the fillets were put off, and the remaining food was eaten by the assemblage, which then dispersed. Tabakea in myth was the father of Na Areau as well as Auriaria, and throughout the Gilbert Islands he is closely associated with the origin of fire, There is also evidence to show that he was one of the gods of the aboriginal race - the dark-skinned people who were settled in the Gilberts before the fairer people from the West invaded them.

Tabakea in myth was the father of Na Areau as well as Auriaria, and throughout the Gilbert Islands he is closely associated with the origin of fire. There is also evidence to show that he was one of the gods of the aboriginal race - the dark-skinned people who were settled in the Gilberts before the fairer people from the West invaded them. The invocation of Tabakea came nearer to the idea of a tribal cult than any other. It was resorted to on occasions of stress, disease or necessity, when not only a single *utu*, but a group of *utu* allied for political or warlike purposes, felt the approach of common danger.

The Kabubu first-fruits ritual

After the pandanus harvest which, in a normal season, occurs during September-October, it was formerly forbidden to partake of any product of the new crop until first-fruits had been offered up and ritual meal eaten at the *boua* of the ancestral deity of the totem-group. The clans of Karongoa, Ababou and Maerua made the offering to the Sun and Moon, but included the names of Auriaria and other ancestral deities in the dedicatory formula. Other social group offered the first-fruits direct to their ancestral deities. The *boua* of the Karongoa group on Marakei - now, most its kind, unhappily destroyed by Christian inconoclasts - was an upstanding monolith of coral rock hewn from the reef and planted in the ground to eastward of the village of Rawanaaui.

As described by elders who, in pre-Christian days, actually performed the clan-rituals, it 'stood as high as a man's shoulder' and was about as 'broad and thick as a man'; it was, moreover, waisted like a man in the middle, though it seems to have had no definitely marked head. This monolith stood in the centre of a circle of flat stones set edgewise in the ground, so as to form a kerb about a hand's breadth high. The diameter of the circle was, according to the account, 'three or four paces'; its exact size was not, as it would seem, a matter of importance. The space within the circle was dressed with white shingle, and therein were buried the skulls of successive generations of clan elders, all males. The crania of the skulls remained uncovered by shingle, so that they might be anointed with oil on occasions when the cult of the ancestral deity was being observed. Care was taken to avoid burying any skulls due west of the *boua*, as this portion of the circle was reserved for food offerings.

For all everyday and overt purposes, including the normal cult of the ancestor, the *boua* represented the body of an ancestral being named Teweia. But for the particular and secret purpose of the first-fruits ritual, it represent4ed no longer Teweia, but the spirit Auriaria. Upon its crest were then perched three red coral blocks, each about the size of two fists, one on top of the other. This addition was known as the *bara* (hat) of Auriaria.

The date of the first-fruits offering was the second day of the next new moons after the pandanus harvest had been gathered.

The hour of the ritual was sunset, when both luminaries were seen together in the sky, the moon setting almost together with the sun.

The material of the offering was a ball of the sweet food called *te korokoro* made of boiled coconut toddy and that desiccated pandanus product called *te kabubu*. The *kabubu* used for the purpose was, of course, manufactured from the newly harvested crop.

The ball of *korokoro* was carried tot eh *boua* by the senior male of the Karongoa clan, all the other men and women of the group following him. The leader wore upon his head a fillet of coconut leaf. Arrived at the place of offering, the whole company assumed the sitting posture adopted by the performer of the fructification ritual; with backs to the sunset and faces to the stone. The leader took his place a little in advance of the others, right up against the kerb of the circular enclosure. Being seated in the ritual posture, he leaned forward and set the ball of *korokoro* at arm's length before him on the shingle near the base of the stone. Throwing back his head to gaze into the sky immediately above the *boua*, and laying his open hands palms upward on the ground by his knees, he intoned:

Kana-mi aei, Taai ma Namakaina,	*This is your food, Sun and Moon,*
Ba ana moan nati Nei Kaina-bongibong.	*Even the first child of the Woman Pandanus-in the twilight.*
Auriaria, ma Nei Tewenei, ma Riiki, ma anti-n rabaraba-ni karawa,	*Auriaria and Nei Tewenei and Riiki, and spirits of the hidden places of heaven,*
	This is your food,
	Even the first young bloom of the magic tree in the twilight.

Kana-mi aei Ba moan tabaa-n te bita-bongibong. Te mauri ao te raoi. Te mauri naba Ngaira-o-o-o!	*Prosperity and peace. The prosperous indeed are we-o-o-o!*

The formula was recited three times. Through the entire ritual that followed, the leader never for a moment ceased to look up into the sky above the stone. Leaning forward, he first groped for the ball of *korokoro* and, having taken it upon the palm of his left hand, returned to an upright posture. Still sitting, he plucked out with his right finger-tips a piece of the sticky ball and moulded it into a pellet, which he then laid on the shingle before the stone as 'the portion of the Sun and Moon and Auriaria'.

This was called the *taarika*. The first portion having thus been given, the proceeded to mould a series of similar pellets, passing each one as it was made back over his right shoulder, where it was taken by the man behind him, and sent along the ranks of sitting people, until every member of the company had a portion. Absolute silence was observed until the *bai-ia*' ('There hands are all full'). Thereupon the leader made for himself a pellet of the food, and raised it in his right hand above his still upturned face, *boua*, and lifted their right arms in a similar attitude. Having allowed time enough for everyone to adopt this posture, the performer dropped the pellet into his mouth and swallowed it whole. The company followed suit. It was essential to the ritual that the bolus should not be bitten.

After a short pause with arm still uplifted, the leader, imitated by the whole assembly, dropped hand to side and turned his face to the ground. The 'looking downward' lasted for a few seconds only. Finally, the leader arose and, without special ceremony, placed whatever remained of the ball of *korokoro* up against the *boua*, beside the small *taarika*, for the remnant (*nikira*) was also the 'portion of the Sun, the Moon and Auriaria'. In a lesser degree also, this *nikira* belonged to the other ancestral spirits, Riiki, Nei Tewenei, Nei Tituaabine, together with the ghosts of those clan elders whose skulls were buried by the *boua*.

Before leaving the spot, the leader anointed with oil and crania of the buried skulls and, after he had performed this rite, any other member of the group might do likewise, choosing at the pleasure any or all of the skulls for anointment.

Fellowship of Skulls

The removal of the skull from the grave, mother, grandfather or grandmother was universal in the Gilberts. The skull was kept on a little mat specially woven for the occasion and was placed on a shelf in the house of the owner. It was considered liable to affront, and was therefore never put on the floor of the house, for fear that in standing above it, a member of the household might insult it with a view of his secret parts. Some households would every day lay a small portion of food on the shelf beside the skull: it was the duty of the closest or the most beloved relative of the deceased to eat this food on his behalf at the day's end. when tobacco was introduced, it became the custom in every island of the Group to allow the skull to share the household pipe.

The skull was held between the palms before the face of the smoker, who inserted the bowl of the pipe into his own mouth and the stem into the jaws of the skull. He then blew down the bowl so that the smoke was driven back through the stem into the gaping jaws. While thus occupied he would address affectionate familiarities to the skull: '*E uara? E kangkang?*' ('How is that? Is it tasty?') and so on.

This sort of conversation was typical of all the relations of the household with the skull. It was a member of the family, as susceptible to offence or pleasure, and as alive to conversations and events beneath the roof, as any human being. It was their friend. while busy about the house a man might throw it an occasional remark as naturally as to his father or brother; or at any time of the day he might take a little oil on his palm and rub it on the cranium of the skull, just as he would perform such an office with smiling yet deferential kindness for one of his living senior relations.

When a particular need made itself felt in the household the help of the deceased ancestor was enlisted through the medium of the skull. The senior living descendant would anoint the cranium with scented oil, and wreaths of flowers would be hung about it. Food would be laid beside it as a *karea* or propitiatory offering and probably a pipe and a stick of tobacco would accompany the food. Just after noon the senior member would lift the skull from its shell and elevate it above his face between his palms: then drawing it close to his cheek he would whisper into its ear the special request that he wished to make on behalf of his people.

A whole *utu* might be gathered together in the *maneaba* to appeal for the ancestor's protection, or a single individual might go informally and without its ear whatever small request he had to make. Sometimes the ancestor would appear in a dream to one of the descendants and would tell him a form of words with which his ghost might be made to converse in whistling noises. The owner of such a charm would generally keep it needed by the household, he would consent to call on the ancestral ghost and ask it the desired question. The skull was the intermediary through which the ghost was called. Offerings were made to it by the *ibonga* or medium, and it was anointed by him with oil in the usual manner. Then he lifted it from its place and whispered into its ear:

O-o! N na wewete-ia Toaakai

O-o! I shall call him, Toaakai

mai aba-na, mai aba-na; e a roko, ba

from his land, from his land, he arrives, for

e a roko ni maneaba-ra aio, be a roko!

he arrives in our maneaba, here, for he arrives!

Soon the ghost would make his presence known by a gentle whistling under the ridge pole of the *maneaba*. It was the function of the *ibonga* to interpret the sounds made to the onlookers. The ghost would answer in this musical language all the questions put to him -

the belief being that if an answer proved afterwards to be wrong, it was certainly the fault of the *ibonga* and not the ghost.

Sometimes this species of oracle became so famous for its infallibility that people of other households and *utu* came to consult it. They would bring propitiatory offerings of food and tobacco to the *ibonga,* who after giving the moan *tiba* (the first share) to the skull would keep the rest as payment. In this way an ancestral ghost would obtain prestige and reverence outside the circle of his own *utu*.

Te Binekua

There is an *utu* of Kuma on Butaritari which claims the power of *Te Binekua* - calling the porpoises. This *utu* belongs to Mone, the land under the sea. When a member dies, he does not go to the land of Bouru or Matang, to which other people go, but to Mone, his spiritual home. The magic connected with Te Binekua, as that concerning navigation, may be inherited by women as well as men. Those who have the power can bring porpoises to shore at any season of the year. Having been asked by the High Chief to call a shoal, the 'caller' lies down in his hut with feet to westward and passes into a natural sleep. While he is asleep his spirit is said to quit his body and go westward to the islet of Bikaati, where it dives under the sea, straight down to the spiritual replica of Bikaati in Mone.

Here live the porpoises. When the caller's spirit comes among them, they are men in the bodies of men, and wear men's clothing. They greet him kindly, and their King receives him as one of that *utu*. After feasting and talking with the people, he begs the King that some of them may accompany him ashore to the *maie* (game or dance). The King permits this, and those who will, arise from the assembly, go to a sandspit a little distance apart, and doff all their clothes. Immediately their garments fall from them they are transformed into porpoises.

All set out together for the village of Kuma, the 'caller' leading them with dancing movements. When they are well on their way, the 'caller' leaves them and hurries back to his sleeping body. His eyes open, he awakes from sleep and says to the people who await him: '*Ea tau, a roko raomi, nako ni katauraoa te maie.*' The whole village, both members and non-members of the *utu*, then goes and decks itself out with mats, garlands and scented oils, exactly as if a dance were toward. The whole company then repairs to the beach. While awaiting the porpoises it is strictly forbidden to talk or even think of food. The porpoises must be referred to as 'our friends', their visit is alluded to as a gathering to the 'dance'. If there is any mention of a killing, the porpoises will hear and turn away in fear.

The animals swim straight to the beach, the 'caller' standing knee deep in the shoal water to welcome them. He goes through the gesture of the dance and repeats the invitation of Te Binekua, then entreats 'his brothers' the porpoises to come and 'dance' ashore. When the creatures are in close, the whole population descends into the sea. Each one chooses a porpoise and standing beside it fondles it, then leads it ashore.

This is the legend first heard from Kitiona of Butaritari and . 'Whatever may be the truth of the caller's descent into Mone,' he continues, 'there is no doubt at all that if you ask one of this *utu* to call the porpoises, they can be made to arrive that very day.'

Maneaba

The Gilbertese (I-Kiribati) *maneaba* is the centre of communal life, the council chamber, the dance hall, the feasting place of the gathered totem groups comprising any local population. As such, it is sacrosanct; no brawling or dispute may take place under its roof, or upon the *marae* (open space) of which it is the centre; its supporting pillars may not be struck; and only games of a definitely religious or social significance (including above all the dance) may be played within its precincts.

The building is susceptible of offence, and may not be spoken of in jest; he who offends it becomes *maraia* and liable to sudden death or sickness. It consists of an enormous thatched roof, whereof the eaves descend to within six feet or less of the ground, supported upon studs or monoliths of dressed coral rock. The largest of these buildings in existence (early 20th century), has an interior length of 120 ft. a breadth of 75 ft., and a height from floor to ridge-pole of 45 ft. There are three main types of *maneaba*: that called Tabiang, whereof the breadth if equal to about half the length; that called Tabontebike, or Te Tabanin which is four-square; and that called Maunga-tabu, whose breadth is to its length in the proportion of about 2.5. All have hipped or gabled, not conical, roofs.

Maneaba

Each totem-group has its hereditary *boti* (sitting-place) in the *maneaba*, and its peculiar functions or privileges in connection with the building of the edifice, or its maintenance, or the ceremonials which take place beneath its roof. To usurp the *boti*, privilege or function of another group is to become *maraia*. Te Maunga-tabu maneaba is called by the Karongoa group 'the enclosure of the Sun and Moon', and the Sun is believed to take vengeance upon any who violate or offend its precincts. Supporting the roof-plate in the middle of the eastern side of this building is a stud named 'Sun', against which the people of Karongoa-n-uea (Karongoa-of-Kings) have their hereditary sitting place. Opposite the 'Sun', in the middle of the western side, is the stud named 'Moon', against which the clans of Ababou and Maerua are seated. Karongoa, Ababou and Marua have the Sun-totem in common and share the monopoly of the Sun-Moon fructification ritual.

All ceremonial and all speech in the Maunga-tabu maneaba are subservient to the will of Karongoa-n-uea, as enunciated by the senior male of the group. This individual is called 'Sun in the *maneaba*', and it is believed that the Sun will pierce the navel of any who contradicts him, questions his judgment, expresses the least doubt about his rendering of a tradition, or attempts to usurp any of his privileges within the sacred building. The Karongoa-n-uea spokesman wears privileges within the sacred building. The Karongoa-n-uea spokesman wears on his head a fillet of coconut leaf called *buna-n Taai* (the fillet of the Sun). On ceremonial occasions he sits alone, slightly in advance of his fellow clansmen, and opens proceedings - after silence has been called - by muttering the magico-religious formula called *te taemataao*, 'to clean the path of his words', and so protect him from interruption or contradiction.

The formula is recited three times with the head bowed, while the hands are slowly rubbed together, palm on palm; after three repetitions, the performer thrown his hands forward, palms up, elbows against body, and raising his head exclaims, '*E oti Taai*' ('the sun appears') or '*Aria-ia ba ti na ongo*' ('take it up for we will hear'), after which the ceremonial or debate proceeds.

The sib of Karongoa-raereke is the companion and acolyte of Karongoa-n-uea in the Maunga-tabu building; its members carry messages from the sacred clan to other groups and, in the Northern Gilberts, its elder 'lifts the word from the mouth of Karongoa-n-uea', i.e., announces to the assembly the whispered oration or judgment of the Karongoa-n-uea spokesman. The privilege of Karongoa-raereke is to take a share of the first portion of any feast, which is the perquisite of Karongoa-n-uea. Its duty is to supervise the laying and maintenance of the coconut-leaf mats (*inaai*) with which the floor of the *maneaba* is covered, and to perform magico-religious rituals for preventing dissension in the sacred edifice. The time for such rituals is the hour when the Sun is approaching his zenith; and among the material used is a *kuo-n-aine* - a cup made of half a coconut shell wherein oil has been boiled. This vessel is said to have formed the magic boat of the Sun-child Bue, ancestor of the Ababou clan, on the voyage to the Sun.

Ababou and Maerua

The Ababou and Maerua groups claim both the Sun and the Moon as their totems, and are seated about the stud called 'Moon' in the middle of the western side of the *maneaba*. The ceremonial function of Ababou is to separate the first portion of Karongoa-n-uea from any food brought to the *maneaba* for the purpose of a feast, and to hand it over to Karongoa-raereke for conveyance to the sacred clan.

The clan of Te Wiwi claims the function of blowing the conch (*bu*) which announces a gathering in the *maneaba*. Members of the Keaki group have the right to prior entry into the building, in the sense that when one or more of them arrives in a crowd at the *marae* upon which the maneabea stands, their companions of other clans (excepting Karongoa-n-uea) will stand aside to let them pass.

The elder of the Tabukaokao group supervises the collection of food for any feast, in the middle of the *maneaba*, and shares with the elder of Ababou the right of dividing it into two equal portions - one for the northern the other for the southern half of the building. Ababou then separates from the northern half the first portion of Karongoa-n-uea,, which is issued before any further distribution is made. Karongoa-raereke carries the first portion to Karongoa-n-uea, and other specific groups have the right of dividing and distributing the remainder.

Outside the *maneaba*, Ababou and Maerua claim the power of making and unmaking eclipses of the sun or Moon, of rain-making, and raising or stilling the wind. These powers are said to be inherited from the hero Bue who was a child of the Sun by a virgin mother. But the Sun's greatest gift to Bue was the craft of building *maneabas*: 'The *maneaba* of Kings, which is called Te Namakaina (Moon); and that called Te Tabanin (The Foursquare); and the *maneaba* whereof the breadth is greater than the length, called Te Ketoa'. It is by virtue of this gift that the clans of Ababou and Maerua lay claim to what is their pre-eminent function, namely that of being, on behalf of Karongoa-n-uea, the master-architects of the Maunga-tabu building.

Their duties in this direction are to find a suitable site for the edifice, to lay out its ground plan, to order the position of all its timbers, and with their hands to cap its ridge with a covering of plaited leaf or matting. Their acolytes in these works are the Eel=totem group of Nukumauea and the Crab-totem group of Tabukaokao. In all their building rituals, the names of Sun and Moon are pre-eminent; they believe that the Sun dwells in the Maunga-tabu *maneaba* because he was the originator of that style of building, and that he will take vengeance upon any person who either offends the edifice or attempts to usurp the functions of imitate the rituals of the builder-clans.

The posts of dressed coral which support the roof of the Maunga-tabu are not up to the accompaniment of a Sun formula. The first timbers to be cut and dressed are the *tatanga* (roof-plates). The heavy work is done by the acolyte Eel and Crab totem groups, but before the dressing of the rough logs begins they are heaped in a pile for ritual treatment by the master-architect of Ababou. Before noon, on a day when the sun and moon are seen together in the sky, the master mounts the pile and, facing east, taps one of the logs lightly with an adze, intoning:

Ba N nangi tiba koroi-a, tatanga-ni maneaba-ia Taai, Namakaina;	*For the time has come for me to cut the roof-plate of the maneaba of the Sun and Moon;*
Ba maneaba-ia Auriaria, Nei Tewenei, Riiki, Nei Tituaabine.	*Even the maneaba of Auriaria, Nei Tewenei, Riikii, Nei Tituaabine.*
E toki tera? E toki te	*What ceases? Violence ceases.*
	What ceases? Evil magic ceases.

bakarere.	*What ceases? Being under a curse ceases.*
E toki tera? E toki te kai-n-anti.	
	What ceases? Being smitten ceases.
E toki tera? E toki te maraia.	
	It ceases, it ceases, it ceases, it ceases.
E toki tera? E toki te tiringaki.	
	Prosperity and peace.
Etoki-i-i, e toki-e-e-e,	
Te mauri ao te raoi.	

The cutting of the rafters and other scantlings is precluded by exactly the same ritual and formula, the word *tatanga* (roof-plate) being replaced by the appropriate term. When the thatch is complete, the ridge capping is laid in position and, again before noon, both sun and moon being seen in the sky, the master-architect mounts the roof armed with a thatching awl. Sitting on the ridge facing east, midway between the gable ends, he stabs the capping with his awl on either side of him and intones:

Ba N nangi tiba ewari-a,	*For I am in the act of piercing it,*
Taubuki-n uma-ia Auriaria, Nei Tewenei, Riiki ma Nei Tituaabine.	*The ridge of their dwelling, Auriaria, Nei Tewenei, Riiki and Nei Tituaabine.*
Ririka-n uma-u tera? Te karau.	*The covering of my dwelling from what? From rain.*
Ririka-n uma-u te buaka;	*The covering of my dwelling from storm (or strife),*
Ririka-n uma-u karawa;	
Ba rokiroki-n uma-ia Taai ma Namakaina.	*The covering of my dwelling from heaven;*
Te ririka-e-e, te ririka-o-o!	*Even the screening in the house of the Sun and the Moon.*
	The covering-e-e, the covering-o-o!

This formula having been recited three times, the master architect descends, and the ridge-capping is sewn in place by workers of Ababou and Maerua. When the work is complete, the officiator again mounts to the ridge, carrying with him four coconuts in their husks. For the purposes of the ceremony these nuts are secretly known as *ata* (human heads). Straddling the north end of the ridge, facing south, he strikes off the proximal end of one nut and, sprinkling its liquor over the capping, mutters in a low voice the following formula three times over:

Bubu-n ai i Aba, bubu-n ai i Abaiti,	*Smoke of fire at Aba, smoke of fire at Abaiti,*
Bubu-n ai i Maunga-tabu, bubu-n ai i Ababou,	*Smoke of fire at the Sacred Mountain, smoke of fire at Ababou,*
Bubu-n ai irou.	*Smoke of fire with me.*
Timtim te rara:	*Drip-drip the blood:*
Taai, Namakaina-o-o, ko kaakangi kana-m te rara!	*Sun, Moon-o-o, thou eatest thy food, the blood!*
Matu, matu, anti ni kamaamate;	*Sleep sleep, spirits of killing;*
Matu, matuy, anti ni kaaoraki;	*Sleep, sleep, spirits of sickness;*
Matu, matu, anti ni	*Sleep, sleep, spirits of evil dreamings;*

kamibuaka;	*Sleep, sleep!*
Matu, matu!	*Overturned is the ...*
Baraaki te unene,	*For the land gives birth.*
B'e bung te aba.	

Proceeding now to the middle of the ridge, he repeats the same ritual, facing first east and then west, using his second and third 'heads'. He finishes at the south end, facing north, using the fourth head.

As each head is emptied of its blood, it is allowed to roll down the thatch of the *maneaba* to the ground below, where its position is anxiously noted. If the majority of *ata* lie with the open end (corresponding to the neck of a human head) pointing towards the *maneaba*, it is a sign of good fortune; but war, sickness or famine are prognosticated if the distal ends are presented to the building.

Art

Architecture of Kiribati

Kiribati's traditional architecture is simple and limited. Most buildings were made of wood, stood a couple feet off the ground, and had thatched roofs. These houses were small, but most villages also had community houses where the people could gather. Beyond these homes, there was little architectural variation in Kiribati prior to the arrival of the Europeans.

With the arrival of the Europeans and missionaries the architecture changed in building materials, techniques, and use. Stronger woods and joining techniques made buildings last longer. New materials, such as bricks were also introduced and are common in the construction of churches, an addition brought by the Europeans and the conversion to Christianity. Other materials, such as concrete and sheet metal are also important as many houses use these materials for construction today.

Today houses and other buildings use more western materials to construct buildings and some European or international styles have also made their way to Kiribati. This is especially true in urban centers, such as Tarawa.

History

The first settlers in the Gilbert Islands and Banaba came from Southeast Asia, by way of Micronesia, some 4,000 to 5,000 years ago. About the 14th century ce the southern islands received an influx of Samoans, and soon thereafter the islanders adopted a gerontocratic style of government (i.e., based on rule by elders). The Line and Phoenix islands had no prehistoric population.

Spanish explorers sighted some of the islands in the 16th century, but most of Kiribati was not charted until the early 19th century, when first whalers and then coconut oil traders reached the islands. From the mid-19th century, Gilbert Islanders were recruited to work on plantations elsewhere in the region.

The Gilbert Islands became a British protectorate in 1892, and Banaba was annexed in 1900 after the discovery of its rich phosphate deposits. Both were linked with the Ellice Islands (now Tuvalu) as the Gilbert and Ellice Islands Colony from 1916; the colony subsequently was extended to include most of the Phoenix and Line island groups and, for a time, Tokelau. Administration was through island governments, which sometimes became enmeshed in sectarian rivalries between Roman Catholics and Protestants. As a response to drought and perceived overpopulation in the 1930s, a resettlement plan was initiated for the Phoenix Islands; under a later plan, other islanders were resettled in the Solomon Islands.

During World War II the islands were occupied by Japan, which was later ejected by Allied forces. The colony had few services until aid-funded development programs were introduced after the war. An elected House of Representatives was established in 1967. The subsequent emergence of ethnic tensions led to the division of the Gilbert Islands and the Ellice Islands into two territories in 1975–76. In 1971 the Banabans sued the British government for a greater share of royalties from phosphate mining and compensation for the island's environmental devastation. The trial ended inconclusively and without a court order to have the mining company restore the land, the outcome for which the Banabans had hoped. In 1981 the community agreed to Britain's offer of a one-time trust payment of $10 million (Australian) in return for the abandonment of further litigation. The Gilbert Islands achieved independence under the name Kiribati in 1979.

After independence a high priority was given to economic development, especially the exploitation of marine resources and the use of the country's strategic position astride the Equator for space launch and tracking projects. Both Japan and China constructed Earth-satellite telemetry stations in the late 1990s, although China dismantled its facilities after Kiribati shifted its formal recognition of China to Taiwan in return for economic assistance in 2003. A commercial satellite-launch platform located on a converted oil-drilling rig east of Kiritimati began operation in the late 1990s. Kiribati belongs to the Pacific Islands Forum, the International Whaling Commission, the Commonwealth, and the United Nations.

In the late 20th and early 21st centuries, rising sea levels (thought to be a result of climate change) threatened to contaminate and eventually submerge Kiribati's low-lying islands. The government investigated strategies for preparing the country for the future and ensuring citizens' future safety. Possible long-term solutions include encouraging skilled workers to emigrate as well as purchasing land elsewhere in the Pacific and creating artificial islets in the ocean similar to offshore oil-drilling platforms to which the population could be moved should some or all of the islands of Kiribati become uninhabitable. In 2014 the government bought some 8 square miles

(20 square km) of land on the Fijian island of Vanua Levu that could serve as a new homeland if one became necessary and that in the interim could be used for supplemental food production.

National Identity. Precolonially, the people of the Tungaru islands formed small, shifting political units, and there was no unified economic or political system or cultural identity. A single national identity emerged only after World War II as a result of colonial policies intended to move the area toward political independence.

Differences between the northern, central, and southern islands of Tungaru, especially in terms of social and political organization, traditions, and group characteristics, are clearly identified by I-Kiribati and underlie national politics. Traditionally, the north had a more complex social organization with a kingship and chiefly classes compared with the more egalitarian social structure of the south. Currently the north and central islands are seen as more progressive than the south, which is more politically and socially conservative.

Ethnic Relations. I-Kiribati can be considered culturally and ethnically homogeneous, with a shared genetic history, cultural traditions, values, historical experience, and language. I-Kiribati distinguish themselves from neighboring island groups and see the greatest conceptual divide between themselves and I-Matang

("Westerners"). The culture and language of Banaba are basically I-Kiribati. The primary issue in Banaban independence movements has been the distribution of phosphate revenues, not cultural differences.

Urbanism, Architecture, and the Use of Space

Rural houses usually are built of traditional materials and are open-sided rectangular structures with thatched roofs and raised floors. In towns, more houses are built with imported materials such as concrete block and corrugated iron. The most symbolically important structure is the rectangular, open-sided maneaba (meeting house), which may be owned by a family, church community, or village. The maneaba functions as a central place for formal and informal group activities. Maneaba built with modern materials follow the traditional prescriptions of style, aspect, and orientation. The floor is composed of unmarked but known sitting places termed boti arranged around the perimeter, with one belonging to each family represented in the maneaba; this is the place from which a representative (usually the oldest male) of each family participates in community discussions and decision making. Churches are architecturally European and often are the largest structures in a village.

In More Detail

The early settlers to Kiribati had a difficult existence since the islands are coral reefs so there are few options in terms of plant and animal life. This made survival very difficult as most people developed a lifestyle focused on the seas and the little the lands offered. Even today the people remain tied to the lands and seas in many ways, but technology, particularly transportation, has made life today much easier as the people have access to numerous goods.

Despite the challenges associated with survival, the people created a lifestyle based on the world around them and slowly developed a unique culture. Although most people are primarily ethnically and linguistically Melanesian, nearly everyone has some Polynesian ancestry and the Polynesians also strongly influenced their culture. Due to heavy contact with the Tongans and other Polynesian people, the culture that developed on the islands was more similar to that of Polynesia than that of Melanesia, although this varied from island to island in this far-stretching archipelago country.

Even with the arrival of Europeans to the South Pacific, there was little immediately impact on the culture of Kiribati, although many people did die due to European diseases. The Europeans had little interest in colonizing or settling these coral reefs so primarily left the people alone. However, many Europeans and Americans stopped on expeditions, particularly whaling expeditions, slowly introducing the people to new technologies and a changing lifestyle. In a more dramatic fashion, missionaries arrived to the islands and converted many people to Christianity. This changed the culture in many ways, from the obvious like building and attending church to a change in clothing as the people became more modest.

In the 1900s the culture continued changing, particularly due to American, British, and other European influence. The country was also formed, uniting various island chains that had many similarities in culture, language, and lifestyle, but were never truly one. Since this time the people have created a more unified culture and lifestyle, which shares similarities and incorporates new technology and communication. However, for many people their culture begins with their local community, island, or island chain and for all of these people their culture and lifestyle remains rooted in their Melanesian and Polynesian past.

In reality, it's unknown when the first people arrived to the modern day islands of Kiribati (pronounced "KIRR-i-bas"). Some estimates say the islands have only been inhabited since 1300 AD, but most estimates believe people arrived much earlier, in fact as early as

3000 BC, although this seems to be a bit early. Although this is a huge window, it seems people most likely arrived to the islands of Kiribati between about 1000 BC and 1000 AD, but little archeological work has been done to provide a more accurate date.

The origin of these earliest immigrants is also unknown, but the people were likely of Austronesian descent. If this is the case the people probably arrived from nearby Micronesia including what are today the Marshall Islands and the Federated States of Micronesia.

The people likely first settled the Gilbert Islands in the west then moved east. The culture and lifestyle of these early settlers was likely based on survival as the people lived off the lands, little of which was fertile, and the seas, which were home to numerous animals and hence food; the rains were heavy so they regularly had fresh water. Beyond this little is known of the culture of the people prior to European arrival.

Despite being an island chain, which essentially isolated the people, other people arrived to the islands sometime in early history. Despite having no written records, it appears the Samoans, Tongans, and Fijians all invaded or visited the islands prior to the 1600s. The Samoans and Tongans introduced aspects of Polynesian culture and the Fijians introduced aspects of a still developing Melanesian culture. Today most people have traces of these ethnic groups in them and there are words and other cultural aspects from Polynesia and Melanesia in Kiribati, meaning these foreigners and locals likely intermarried.

The first Europeans arrived in the 1500s or 1600s, although settlement wasn't the objective at the time. These early arrivals were simply explorers or merchants, most commonly whalers. Perhaps the most significant of these explorers were John Marshall (after whom the Marshall Islands are named) and Thomas Gilbert from the United Kingdom, after whom the Gilbert Islands are named, who came in 1788. However, few of these early people made any impact on the culture until the 1800s when greater numbers of people began to arrive to the islands. During this time the islands were often used as a stopping point for traders in the Pacific Ocean. Again colonization and settlement weren't the objectives at the time, but people became exposed to numerous European diseases, killing huge portions of the population. These outside influences also introduced new tools, technology, and other small aspects of outside culture. All of this also stirred up local battles between tribes on the numerous islands.

As the lives of the people in Kiribati slowly changed in the 1800s, the people of the Gilbert Islands and of the Ellice Islands (Tuvalu) agreed to become a protectorate of the British Empire in 1892. Nine years later the island of Banaba was added to this protectorate when the British discovered phosphate on the island. This was truly an economic union as the people of Banaba and the Gilbert Islands were vastly different from a cultural, linguistic, and ethnic perspective. Additionally, the lifestyles were different as Banaba offers a mountainous landscape and great soils, giving the people on that island a very different way of life.

In 1916 a few of the islands in the Line Island chain (in Kiribati's far east) joined this union and later most of the rest of the Line Islands joined as well. All of these islands were eventually incorporated into the British colony called the British Western Pacific Territories. At this time the rest of the Line Islands, as well as the Phoenix Islands fell under the Jurisdiction of the United States.

Throughout this period of British rule foreigners settled the islands, but these islands were never a focus of British colonization and never became a significant immigration destination for the British or other foreign nationals. Because of this, little changed in the culture of the people of Kiribati during these years. The two most significant and longest lasting changes during this time came in the form of technology, such as new communication and transportation, and the introduction of Christianity.

Missionaries from the United Kingdom and other countries arrived to the islands to spread Christianity and they did so very successfully. This was likely the most important change to the people, their lifestyle, and their culture instigated by the British and other foreigners on the islands, including the Americans in the Phoenix Islands and Line Islands.

The primary reason few other cultural changes took place, and the reason few settlers arrived to the islands was that there was no true economic value in the islands. In fact the only island that held true colonial power was Banaba due to the Phosphate deposits. Banaba was the only economic power in the islands, so became home to most of the settlers and trade in the islands. Sadly, these mines were emptied and the foreigners left, leaving behind few changes other than the destruction of the island's lands.

It was also during this time, in 1937, that famed American aviator Amelia Earhart went missing on a flight in the region. It is believed by some that she may have landed and/or crashed on Gardner Island (now known as Nikumaroro), which is in the Phoenix Islands and at the time under the jurisdiction of the United States.

Having little military presence in the islands, when the Japanese arrived in World War II, they easily took over a few of the islands in today's Kiribati, but the British and other Allied forces re-took these lands later in the war as the islands became stepping stones on the path to Japan. Tarawa Atoll was the recipient of one of these battles, which the Allies eventually won as they moved northwest from there.

After the war, Kiribati remained under British control, but by the 1970s independence was becoming more realistic. The Ellice Islands declared independence in 1975, creating the nation of Tuvalu and in 1978 the Gilbert Islands held their first general election, giving this island chain, along with the Line Islands and Phoenix Islands independence in 1979. The British had little interest in maintaining these islands as they had little economic value and few British settlers had called the islands home, so the transition was relatively smooth from the British perspective.

Since independence in 1979 Kiribati has, for the most part, remained politically stable. The only major issue is that the island of Banaba has run out of phosphate and their local economy has essentially crashed. Many of the residents have moved to Fiji and some are actively requesting that the island of Banaba join Fiji. Despite these calls for succession by Banaba, no legislature has been passed to make this move official. Today only about 300 people still live on the island of Banaba.

Tourism

Travel Guide

Straddling the equator and right on the International Dateline, Kiribati (pronounced *Kirimass*) is a nation of 33 widely spread atolls that are good for diving, bird watching and enjoying Micronesian culture. Racked by battle in WWII, ravaged by Cold War thermonuclear devices and spooked by rising sea levels today, this country of low-lying islands is as unique and remote as they come.

The region is comprised of three groups; the Gilberts, where the capital Tarawa is; the Line Islands, site of the famous Christmas Island (not the Australian one); and the lesser known Phoenix group. The most striking feature of Kiribati outside of the white, coral-sand beaches is its profusion of lagoons, which are perfect for diving and bird watching. South Tarawa, Christmas Island, and Kanton Island (of the Phoenix) all have them, though Christmas' is the most sublime and accessible.

Most visitors head out on boating trips, dives or by sea plane to sightseeing over Abaiang and Maiana atolls that depart from Tarawa. However, each group can only be approached via an international flight, or a long time at sea, such as the restricted Phoenix Island Marine Protected Area, which is chiefly accessible by boat from Kanton Island.

The scuba diving in Kiribati is a huge draw, where every type of coral and fish can be seen along with a myriad of WWII wrecks in Tarawa. Game fishing and bird watching abound, particularly on Christmas Island. Other assets include breezy tropical weather, a lack of tourist infrastructure which greatly appeals to the more seasoned traveler and the simple lifestyle of its inhabitants. In contrast, the capital, South Tarawa, is a busy network of islets, but is home to some of the main sights like the Parliament House and WWII guns.

The locals are friendly and welcoming and love to showcase their culture during Island Nights and through their range of handicrafts. The cuisine is largely sea-based and very basic, while expat bars and guesthouses often have Western goodies. The nightlife is low-key, which suits most visitors seeking relaxation, while accommodation, for the most part, tends to be traditional thatched-roof *kiakia* huts.

Kiribati is hardly a value destination mainly due to the cost of getting here though living and eating like a local will help save money.

Getting around Tarawa and Christmas Island is mainly by minibus, but you can rent cars in Kiribati, while ferries and charters run out to neighboring islands within Tarawa. Getting between the atoll groups is more difficult than it seems as the distances are so far. You can't fly between Tarawa and Christmas Island, for example.

Attractions

Kiribati's heart is it's beaches, but the islands of South Tarawa are also known for their history, retaining rusted Japanese guns from WWII and their semi-impressive buildings in the capital. People come all this way mainly for the ecology of the islands and the ecclectic wildlife. Main islands have airports and boat charters.

Tarawa
South Tarawa (consisting of several islets) is the capital of Kiribati, located on an atoll of the same name. Most of the action takes place on the islets of Betio and nearby Bairiki and Bonriki, which lie southwest and are quite densely populated. They are hot and noisy and a launching pad for visits to the other islands. Sights in South Tarawa include the Parliament building, President's Office and the WWII guns used during the Battle of Tarawa along the beaches. You

can get here via Bonriki International Airport located east of Tarawa.

Address: South Tarawa, Gilbert Islands

Christmas Island
Known as Kiritimati Island in the local tongue (which translates to the same thing), Christmas Island is the largest landmass of the archipelago and the world's largest coral atoll. It is all wildlife sanctuary, strewn with ponds and animals. Visitors mainly come for the scuba diving (shipwrecks and coral) and fishing, as well as to view huge colonies of birds. Cruises pull in at London, the main settlement and port. There's also an airport on the island.

Address: Christmas Island, 'Northern' Line Islands

Line Islands
The Line Islands is the largest group in the chain and part of the greater Line Islands that also incorporate some US islands. Christmas Island resides here and is the main landmass of the archipelago. When tourists come, they usually head to Christmas Island first for its tropical beaches, amazing lagoons and salt flats. There's an airport with regular flights to Honolulu. Teraina (Washington) and Tabuaeran (Fanning) are also popular destinations.

Address: Line Islands, Eastern Kiribati

Outer Islands

Though the title would suggest remoteness and they are the Outer Islands are actually part of the main Gilbert chain, so they are closer to Tarawa than the Phoenix or Line Islands. However, for all intensive purposes, they are hardly developed, with only basic guesthouses and small airstrips. Communication with the outside world is a hassle, but this appeals to most visitors as it allows them to completely disconnect and enjoy the idyllic beaches and traditional culture of the locals.

Address: 'Outer' Gilbert Islands

Phoenix Island Marine Protected Area
The Phoenix Islands are comprised of fine beaches and amazing landscapes strewn with blue lagoons in Kiribati. People come here mainly to spy on the extensive bird populations, while beneath the waves is one of the most incredible sights anywhere on earth; masses of coral including lettuce coral. However, these islands are tougher to visit and scuba diving is restricted (typically only allowed via special tours and scientific expeditions).

Address: Phoenix Islands

Ambo Lagoon Club
The Lagoon Club on Ambo Island in South Tarawa is one of the top options for fun in the Gilbert group, especially if you have kids. There are all sorts of water-based activities, including a swimming pool and

lagoon along with a meeting house and bar.

Address: Ambo Island, South Tarawa

Food and Restaurants

Entertainment and dining out are quite low-key in Kiribati and confined to the main towns and villages in hotels and guesthouses. The local cuisine is seafood-based and dishes are somewhat of an acquired taste, with Western menus limited. Note that alcohol is banned in some of the Outer Islands.

Bars and Pubbing in Kiribati

Bars are few and far between, though there are places to kickback on the main islets of Tarawa, and most of the major hotels have some kind of watering hole. Betio has a few of note, including the *Royal Bar* (Central Betio, South Tawara), which is air-conditioned and open until about midnight on weekends and 10:00 p.m. during the week. Another popular spot in Betio is *Captains Bar* (Betio, South Tawara), best known for their monthly weigh-ins of the Betio Game Fishing Club.

Tarawa, the capital, has several spots, including the so-called called kava bars and the *Midtown* (South Tarawa) disco, which is open until late. The *Night Spot* also has a dance floor, while the *Lagoon Club*

(Ambo, South Tawara) is the most popular nightlife option on the islet. On Christmas Island, London is the main settlement, although tourist hotels have the pick of the bars such as in the Captain Cook Hotel.

For local music and dancing, consider attending "Island Nights," which are all about showcasing traditional Micronesian culture.

Dining and Cuisine in Kiribati

I-Kiribati traditional food is based on rice and fish, with the sashimi being as good and as fresh as it gets. The *palu sami* (a coconut cream-curry powder-taro leave-seaweed concoction) is a Kiribati specialty, though visitors may want to try it with chicken or pork as opposed to plain. In the south, be sure to try the *pandanus* fruit with coconut cream.

There's a lack of Western restaurants, although the bigger hotels and guesthouses have full menus, but expect to pay more. Fruits and vegetables are also quite limited and equally pricey, while coconuts are ubiquitous and very nutritious.

There are plenty of eateries in the main towns of Kiribati, including fast food and Chinese restaurants. Bairiki and Betio have several options, including *Amms Restaurant* (Betio, South Tawara),

Matarena's Restaurant(Bairiki, South Tawara) near the wharf and the *Café* (Bairiki, South Tawara). You can also find fish and chips in Betio. The *Ambo Lagoon Club* (Ambo, South Tawara) is good for both eating and drinking and has a pool and sports on TV. There's a *maneaba* meeting house here, too, which is good for local feasts and movies.

Shopping and Leisure

Shopping is typically limited to handicrafts in South Tarawa and London, while essentials can be purchased at fruit and vegetable markets. The locals churn out a range of art such as basketry and necklaces, while shark swords make excellent Kiribati souvenirs. You can haggle, but keep in mind that they don't earn much. Most shops are open daily.

There's a supermarket on Bairiki islet in South Tarawa where most people stock up on all their regular groceries. It has both fresh and frozen foods as well as dairy and fruit and is open every day. Fern is another popular shop in Tarawa, which is good for pies and wine.

Kiribati Handicrafts

There are several handicraft shops on South Tarawa where everything from basic baskets and fans made from *pandanus* leaves are sold, to coconut shells, seashell necklaces, model canoes, and traditional huts. The Kiribati shark-tooth sword which has sharks teeth embedded in decorated coconut wood is the prize item, though most are copies. Try the RAK Handicraft Centre (Tangintebu, Tarawa) or the Itoiningaina Handicraft Center (Teaoraereke, Tarawa) for more authentic varieties.

Transportation

Kiribati Taxis and Car Rental

There are no actual taxis in Kiribati, with private minibuses being the main form of public transportation on South Tarawa and Christmas Island. These minbuses (usually red or white) typically run on a shared system and are hailed at random. They will also drop off anywhere; you simply need to shout *i-kai!* (stop). They are relatively cheap, though Christmas Island is naturally more expensive. They can also be chartered as a taxi by calling in advance. *Utirerei* (+686 22 530) is based in Ambo and serves South Tarawa.

Cars can be rented in South Tarawa and Christmas Island and hotels can provide vehicles at rates slightly more than in the US. You'll need an International Driving Permit (IDP) and they drive on the left in Kiribati. Roads are in good condition, although potholes and speed bumps are frequent. There's a small toll across the causeway to Betio islet.

Kiribati Water Taxis

Cruises stop at Tarawa (Gilbert Islands), Christmas Island (Line Islands) and remote Banaba, while Fanning Island (one of the lesser visited Line Islands) is served by Norwegian. Passenger ferries run between the Gilbert Islands, chiefly from Betio to some of the Outer Islands (southern Gilbert), like Maiana and Kuria, as well as up to Abaiang and Marakei in North Tarawa. This service is operated by Supercat, but is sketchy in the wet season.

Charters also run these routes, and between islands within other groups, but getting between groups such as from Gilbert to the Line Islands is best done by flying from Fiji or Hawaii. Note: the Line Islands are particularly spread out; sometimes by as much as several hundred miles between atolls.

Kiribati Trains and Buses

There is no railway in Kiribati, and the bus service is simply shared minivans that double as charter taxis. They run between the towns of South Tarawa, as well as on Christmas Island from about 6:00 a.m. to 9:00 p.m. Services are frequent and cheap. There is no bus service outside Tarawa (including the Outer Islands) or Christmas Island, however; you can rent a truck or motorcycle.

Things to do

There are many adventures to be had on and around the islands that make up the nation of Kiribati. In a nation with the biggest water to land ratio in the world, water is a dominant feature in the lives of the I-Kiribati, and for all visitors.

Fishing is world class – centred on Kiritimati (Christmas) Island, one of the few places in the world you can saltwater fly fish, for the mighty fighting bone fish! The deeper waters around Kiritimati and the Gilbert Islands are also great places for record breaking game fishing.

For those looking for some culture, there is plenty to see and do around the island. **Culture** in Kiribati is still very uncommodified – the best way to experience a relatively untouched culture is to take a domestic flight or ferry across to an outer island and meet the ever friendly local people. If you come at the right time of year you may also be able to witness local celebrations, in religious holidays such as Easter or Christmas; or national celebrations such as Kiribati Independence. If you would like to take a bit the culture home with you, there amazing handicrafts for sale, still made the traditional way.

The Gilbert group of islands host a number of *World War II historical sites*. Tarawa, Makin (now called Butaritari), Abemama (also the ocean island of Banaba) were invaded by the Japanese in 1941, just after they bombed Pearl Harbour. After the Japanese fortified the atolls, In 1942 and 1943 US Marines conducted a number of large scale raids to remove the Japanese presence. Today, relics of the battles and forts can be visited.

Kiribati is also host to the Phoenix group of islands – including the *Phoenix Islands Protected Area (PIPA)*, the world's largest marine protected area. For bird lovers, this area hosts nesting and feeding grounds for 19 species of wild sea birds. For those that like it underwater, a vast playground hosting a rich diversity of fish (509 identified species) and other marine life (mammals, sharks, invertebrates, plant life) in plentiful numbers in windward, leeward and lagoon habitats.

If you like it on top of the water, there is amazing *surf breaks* off Fanning island.

We also have a number of tours and other outdoor activities – if your in Kiribati on business or just wanting to explore, there is a range of day and weekend package tours available. Why not let others organise the schedule, and let a local show you around!

To experience our culture and lifestyle will be a memory you will have for the rest of your life. The culture of Kiribati is complex and diverse, with each island having its own unique ways. Though a living body, many people remain true to the century old traditions and practices that define what it means to be I-Kiribati.

Cultural practices such as community meetings under the maneaba (traditional meeting house) to socialize and feast (a botaki), respect of elderly people, guest hospitality and importance of family remain important facets in the culture of Kiribati.

We warmly welcome visitors in many of our customs and activities, and are proud of our way of life and its celebration. The way of living is very simple and people plan theirliving for a day only, without worrying about their future, living with the moto "Tomorrow is another day". Survival revolves around strength, motivation and ambition to live within that particular day. Daily lives revolve around the rise and fall of the tide, dictating fishing conditions and timing and availability of transport. Sustanance is from the coconut and breadfruit trees, and the ocean.

The traditional dances of Kiribati are a unique form of art and expression. The movement of the feet, hands and of course the whole body imitates the movement of the frigate birds while walking and flying. The costumes are made out of local materials. The frigate bird symbolizes many important things in the traditional living context of the I-Kiribati. It provides navigation to fishermen while lost at sea, provides weather information for the people and also gives a sign of peace and harmony.

Visitors can experience I-Kiribati culture in many shapes and forms. However we do recommend the best way is to take the plunge and live on an outer island for a week and to immerse you fully in our daily culture. To plan such a visit we have included a number of suggested itineraries that can help you, as well as a number of fact files on many of Kiribati's outer islands.

The main thing to do in Kiribati is enjoy the beaches and water, with lots of options for swimming, scuba diving and snorkeling. Fishing is also a big deal, with world class bone fishing from the main center of Tarawa. Christmas Island has the best of the diving and fishing, along with great bird watching.

The primary time to enjoy the sea is May through October, when it is calmest and driest. The islands are well equipped for tours, with hotels and independent operators offering trips to dive sites, fishing spots and protected areas for bird watching. For a quintessential Kiribati activity, attend a meeting house (*maneaba*) sit-in to witness stories and dance.

Scuba diving is one of the main attractions of Kiribati and, owing to the remoteness and lack of industrial fishing, the variety of marine life you'll see is staggering. Christmas Island has the best diving on the archipelago, with the *Christmas Island Diver's Association* offering tours to the top sites. Phoenix Island also has good diving, though is restricted. In Tarawa, *Kukurei Dive*, also organizes trips to Ouba. Snorkeling can be arranged from most guesthouses, but avoid the main lagoon at South Tarawa.

The **swimming** is also pleasant wherever you go. The Dai Nippon Causeway at Tarawa is nice on either side, while North Tarawa and the Outer Islands (to the south) are also good for those staying in the Gilbert Islands. Just avoid swimming in South Tarawa's lagoon.

Bird watching is best on Christmas Island, where hundreds of species nest, including migratory seabirds in June and December. There are several nature reserves here namely the Phoenix Island Protected Area where visitors can get up close and personal with a guide. Popular varieties found on Kiribati include the great frigate birds, masked boobies, black noddies, and several types of tern (including fairies). Boats take in the various islets or you can access the secluded sites by truck. All hotels on Christmas Island can arrange tours, including the *Captain Cook Hotel*.

Fishing is a major pastime, which is how the locals survive, living off food from the sea and coconuts mainly. *Kiribati Horizons* can organize tours out to many of the islands, offering lagoon or open-water game fishing. Ambo Island lagoon and Ouba, as well as the Dai Nippon Causeway, are all good areas where tuna and marlin can be snagged, along with amazing bonefish. The best angling, however, is off Christmas Island or Phoenix Island. *Dive & Fishing Adventure Lodge* can also help you arrange charters.

Whale watching is popular December through April with *South Pacific Tour*, where minks, killer whales and dolphins are routinely spotted. Boats can also be rented "with a skipper" for multiday cruises.

Other popular activities in Kiribati include golf on Ambo Island, a links course, and visiting the traditional *maneaba* meeting houses to partake in singing and dancing with the locals.

See more thing to do in detail below:

Wildlife

The number of native plants and animals in Kiribati are very limited since the country is an island nation. Despite its many islands and great length, Kiribati's native land animal life is almost non-existent and the plant life is nearly as absent. The migrating birds and sea life had the most significant presence in creating today's plant and animal life. Much of what is found on the islands today was introduced in pre-historic times by the migrating people, birds, winds, and ocean currents.

As an island nation that rose from the sea floor there were no native mammals in Kiribati, although a few bat species arrived thousands of years ago. Some species of rats also made their way to the islands hundreds, if not thousands of years ago. Other than this, no land mammals existed in Kiribati until the arrival of the earliest people, who brought with them dogs and pigs.

The seas are also home to mammals including dolphins and whales who call the surrounding waters home. These waters are also filled with thousands of fish, shellfish, and other forms of sea life. This sea life includes surgeonfish, clownfish, sailfish, puffer fish, butterfly fish, grouper, barracuda, tuna, snapper, bonefish, mackerel, marlin, mahi-mahi, shrimp, krill, crab, seahorses, manta rays, sharks, jellyfish, starfish, sea urchins, and coral among many others.

The water and the land have attracted more than just fish; they have also attracted numerous birds, including many that feed off the animals in the sea. The bird life in Kiribati includes frigatebirds, doves, parrots, ducks, heron, terns, warblers, pigeons, and cuckoos among others.

Like the mammalian life, the reptilian and amphibious life is fairly limited. The most common of these animals are those adapted to the water and swimming as sea turtles can be found in the nearby waters. Land species have again made their way to the islands in numerous methods and today lizards, snakes, and geckos are among the most common of these animals.

The insect and other small animal life is fairly diverse as many insects can fly or float and have made their way to Kiribati. These animals include butterflies, moths, beetles, bees, ants, flies, snails, spiders, and mosquitos among others.

The plant life, like the animal life, is limited due to geography and climate. The winds and water currents have taken seeds to the islands and in other cases birds have transported seeds to the islands. Because of this, many of the more commonly known plants on the islands today are not actually native to Kiribati, but rather arrived from distant islands like New Guinea and those further west. These plants, or their seeds, arrived with animals, people, winds, and ocean currents from island to island until they reached Kiribati. Plants from these islands, that now thrive in the country, include coconuts, taro, breadfruit, bananas, yams, arrowroot, lemons, and sugarcane among others.

There is also a presence of other trees and plants, including orchids, hibiscus, eucalyptus, frangipani, pawpaw, ferns, mosses, mangrove trees, and pandanus trees.

Bird Watching in Kiribati

Kiritimati Island is a sanctuary and breeding ground in the Pacific for seabirds. With very little land in any direction, Kiritimati supports 18 different species of birds, including the endemic Christmas Island Warbler. The island is also home, and a population stronghold, to the endangered Phoenix Petrel and the White Throated Storm Petrel.

Supporting nine designated protected zones to support the breeding and nesting of the various bird species Kiritimati takes it role in supporting these birds very seriously. The Kiribati Ministry for

Wildlife and Conservation is responsible for ensuring the breeding grounds are not disturbed.

While seabirds can nest and breed throughout the year, as there is little temperature fluctuation, the best breeding seasons are June and December.

In Central Kiribati the Phoenix Island Protected Area also supports an extensive bird colony and nesting habitat. For more information on the Phoenix Island protected area.

Birds found on Kiritimati Island are: phoenix shearwaters, wedge-tailed shearwaters, christmas shearwaters, audubon's shearwaters, polynesian storm petrels, red-tailed tropicbirds, masked boobies, brown boobies, great frigate birds, red-footed boobies, lesser frigate birds, great crested terns, grey backed terns, sooty terns, brown noddies black noddies, blue-gray noddies, and white terns.

To arrange bird watching tours contact your accommodation who can arrange a personalised tour to suit your specific interests.

Diving & Snorkeling

Scuba Diving – Tarawa & Neighbouring Gilbert Island Atolls

Kukurei Dive is the Gilbert Islands newest dive operator. James Smith is a PADI accredited Dive Master and provides an array of diving both in the Tarawa Lagoon and in locations just off neighbouring atolls. Diving packages can be arranged in conjunction with Ouba Islet Resort & Fishing Lodge. With years of experience in diving the islands of Kiribati, James can ensure you get to see the best of Kiribati's underwater playground.

For more information contact:

Mr. James Willie Smith,

Managing Director,

Ocean Flower Underwater World Sight Seeing

Phone: (686) 96545 / 92146

Email: kukureidive@gmail.com

Email: jameswillie.smith2@gmail.com

Diving Packages with Ouba Islet Resort & Fishing Lodge, please contact:

Mr. Emil Schutz

Tel: (686) 26136

Mobile Ph: (686) 90440

Email: schutz@kiribatihorizons.com.ki

Fishing

Fishing in Kiribati - Bone and Sports Fishing

Are you up for the adventure of fishing one of the best fishing locations in the world? Whether you prefer the deep blue waters with big game fish, or prefer the crystalline waters and serenity of saltwater flyfishing, Kiribati is the destination for you. A wise man once said *"Calling fishing a hobby is like calling brain surgery a job"*.

One big reason anglers come to Kiribati though is the mighty bonefish – by fly or saltwater spin, Kiritimati (Christmas) Island is the place to be. There's also some world class game fishing, having obtained many International Game Fishing World Records, the waters in Kiribati are open for international anglers to try their hand. From bonefish, Giant Trevally, to Sail Fish and Marlin, Kiribati won't disappoint.

So why wait – get your friends and mates and make the trip to fishing nirvana – Kiritimati can be accessed via Fiji or Hawaii, while you can get to Tarawa and the Gilbert Islands through Fiji only

Kiritimati (Christmas) Island Fishing

Kiritimati (Christmas) Island is a fisherman's paradise. Situated 1,200km South of Honolulu in the Central Pacific, just north of equator, Kiritimati is the largest coral atoll on the planet where the sea and sky naturally decorate a 250 square miles of white sand, iridescent aqua lagoons, coconut palms and endless flats.

This fishing destination is spectacular because it combines all the elements critical to fly-fishing success. Consistent year-round weather, endless hard sand flats, and magnificent numbers of cruising Bonefish and Trevally- making it ideal for the serious angler. What makes the fishing so special and extraordinary is the natural and raw power of the bonefish – it can fight so hard with so much strength that it makes the anglers work twice as hard. The knowledge of local guides always produces a big difference in fishing as they know their own flats, tides, reefs, waters, and fish. Their eagle eyes can spot the fish in any kind of weather condition.

If you still want more, you can always try your hand at either Blue fin, Golden or Giant Trevally! Giant Trevally is the strongest and powerful species on flats where most fishermen love to challenge its natural power on a 12 weight fly and spinning rod. Many fly and spin fishermen from all over the World come to Kiritimati Island just to wrestle with this powerful fish. The Trevally normally cruise everywhere on flats, inside natural channels, in deep waters inside the lagoon, and offshore along the coastal reefs – they can weight from 10lbs up to more than 100lbs.

Other species such as Sailfish, Wahoo, Barracuda, Sharks, Tuna and Bill fish are always out there in the blue ocean as a fishing bonus.

Fishing Gear to Bring

The best choice for Trevally fishing is 10–12 weights. Sizes of floating lines recommended are the 10-12 weight. Sizes of Monofilament leaders from 80lbs-100 lbs perfectly work in Christmas Island, and leader materials are from 30 down to 12lbs tippets. Trevally flies, popping bugs with kamagazu hooks, streamers, lefty deceivers, rat cliffs are right stuffs for your fishing and do not forget to bring along as well one spinning rod reaches the speed of 5.0 ratio and surface lures to attract big Trevally. We recommend 9-9 ½ foot 7, 8, or 9 weight graphite rods for bonefish and heavier 10-12 weight rods for Trevally. Sage's 890 RPLXi-3 is ideal. Eight weights may be better for beginners but no matter what you experience, bring at least two rods in case you break one. You will also need a reliable saltwater reel like Abel's large arbor Super 8. A bullet proof reel with a smooth friction drag is essential.

More than Fishing

If you have companions and family that don't like fishing as much as you, or you want a break from the fishing, there is always meeting the locals and learning the culture, bird watching, lagoon sightseeing and snorkeling , going to London, Paris and Poland all in one day...are all part of the one week holiday package if you do not fish. These activities are available at lodges and should be a participation of 2-5 people per group.

Travelers are given the opportunity here to explore the beauty of Kiritimati Island and its people and their culture to learn and see for themselves how these people survive and what the island provides for them to live on every day. Activities available include SCUBA diving, wildlife lagoon and snorkel at Paris Point, surfing, bird watching, snorkeling and swimming at Cook Islet Bay, and cultural tours.

Tarawa & Gilbert Islands Fishing

Are you up to the thrill of bringing in a big marlin or sailfish? If so, the Gilbert Islands offer some of the best game fishing in the Pacific. Experienced anglers from Tarawa can take you on a fishing adventure to some of their best fishing spots. Feel the rush of catching sailfish, blue marlin, giant trevally, wahoo, black marlin, yellow fin & dog tooth tuna, and barracuda.

Chartered game fishing trips would cost around AUD$500 to $1000+, inclusive of fishing boat, fuel, fishing gear, and refreshments (beer/soft drinks & packed lunch). Game fishing tournaments are also held in Tarawa, run by the Betio Game Fishing Club every month, with the weigh in hosted at Captains Bar in Betio. Tournaments are timed on the Saturday nearest to the monthly full moon.

Surfing in Kiribati

Big and long breaks off Fanning and Kiritimati (Christmas) islands, the final frontier – where "lack of crowds" is a complete understatement, you will be lucky if anyone else is out with you. This is the beauty of the isolation of the central pacific Of course this exclusiveness is because these places can be a little challenging to get to – however you are in the right place to find out. Only for the truely adventurous surfer/traveller, below are the details you will need to arrange your surf trip of a life time, and waves you have only dreamt about.

Fanning (Tabuaeran) Island

Of all of Kiribati, Fanning is the pick with almost year round consistent swell. Fanning has breaks on the North and South, making the most of both Northern Hemisphere and Southern Hemisphere swells. The two most consistent breaks are 'English Harbour' in the South with strong and consistent March to June; and 'Walers' in the

North with strong conisistent swell from October to March (even picks up some southern swell.

Kiritimati (Christmas Island)

Kiritimati is host to a golden five kilometer stretch of points, reefs and channels between London village and Paris point. This stretch is reputed to have 24 surfable waves – with surf season October through to March. The swell hits Kiritimati about a day or two after it hits Hawaii – a 8' to 12' swell at Sunset Beach in Hawaii will result in 6' to 10' clean faces in Kiritimati one to two days later. Of the 24 breaks, two third are user friendly with deep channels and sand of soft reef bottom. The other third is has rough coral bottoms and are for experienced surfers only.

Tarawa and the Gilberts

Not all of the Gilberts is good for surfing, but there are a few breaks around. If your stopping by Tarawa on a business trip or to visit friends or relatives, there are some decent waves to be found on the end of a rising tide. The most easy to get to breaks are in Temaiku – a village not far from the airport. The best break in Tarawa though is Naa – right at the tip of North Tarawa. After that, there are some breaks off the outer islands – off the Abaiang islets near the Ouba lodge, as well as some of Marakei. These are for only the truely adventurous though – contact our office for more details!

Kiribati Island Tours

Kiritimati Island

On Kiritimati Island, your accommodation provider will be able to arrange whatever tours you would like to undertake. This includes lagoon boating and kayaking, cultural tours to meet the locals, or exploring the amazing Kiritimati Island (actually an atoll) environment. SCUBA Diving and snorkling can be arrange, along with some fantastic birdwatching (as well of course the world class Fishing and Surfing options).

Tarawa and the Outer Gilbert Islands

Tarawa is the base for adventures around the Outer Gilberts, and also hosts some very interesting sites and tours itself. Below are the details of tour providers. For details of tours of the World War II sites, also see our World Ware II page.

Kiribati Holidays Tours

Abatao Cultural Tour

This fascinating tour in Abatao enables you to discover some of the traditional cultural practices of Kiribati that are still continued today. Discover the amazing world of giant clams at a local clam farm and experience a little of the life and customs of a traditional Kiribati village. Among the things that you might see are how garlands are made, how mats are woven and how toddy is cut, among many other things.

North Tarawa Conservation Area Tour

Travel by boat to the North Tarawa Conservation Area, an area looked after by the local I-Kiribati to preserve the environment and culture for future generations. Explore a variety of islets, where you will have the opportunity to discover places of historical significance and hear traditional stories. Visit local traditional buildings, and see the fish traps, watch the traditional sailing canoes and explore the pristine marine waters.

Kiribati Holidays is also able to customize tours and activities to suit your needs and arrange trips to outer islands.

For more information, contact:

Kiribati Holidays
Located in Bikenibeu near the Otintaai Hotel

Tel: (686) 28399 Fax: (686) 28989

Email: info@kiribatiholidays.com

Website: www.kiribatiholidays.com

World War II Sight

The Islands of Kiribati lay claim to a number of the bloodiest battles that were fought out in World War II. Sixty years on and much of the evidence of these battles still remain available for travellers to view as a living museum of this part of history; in particular Tarawa, Butaritari and Abemama of the Gilbert group, and Banaba island.

The Japanese entered the pacific and invaded the Gilberts in December of 1941, two days after they bombed Pearl Harbour. In August of 1942, the US Marines held three major operations in an attempt to remove the Japanese, including "The Battle of Tarawa", reputedly one of the bloodiest battles ever fought in World War II.

On Tarawa and Butaritari Atoll there are still physical relics of the occupation and operations. This includes four eight inch coastal defense guns, and solid concrete bunkers and pillboxes. Rusted tanks, amtracs, ship wrecks, and plane wrecks can also be seen on the shores at low tide. To see these you can just take a walk or bus ride around Tarawa, but we recommend you do a guided tour so you don't miss anything!

Molly's Tours (in Tarawa)

Molly will take you back in time to one of bloodiest battles ever fought during World War II. The tour will be on Betio, the scene of "Operation Galvanic" one of the most significantand bloody battles in the history of WWII. The tour requires that reef shoes are worn as you will be walking out over the reef to see the war relics and artifacts. Highlights of the tour include: Red Beach 1,2 and 3; Vickers 8" coastal guns, brought during the Russian Japanese war of 1905; Japanese bunkers and pillboxes which fortified the island of Betio in 1942; see the remains of Amtracs, American Sherman and Japanese type 95 tanks; American and Japanese memorials, the memorial to the British and New Zealand coastal watchers and the Cenotaph erected as a time capsule to Americans fallen in action; and Buddhist and Shinto shrines erected by the Japanese in memory of their war dead in the Gilbert and Marshall Islands.

Tel/Fax: +(686) 26409

Email: mollybrown413@gmail.com

The Makin Raid and Battle of Makin (Butaritari) Tour

For battle field tour itineraries and accommodation arrangements on Butaritari Atoll please contact:

Kiribati Holidays
Tarawa Office Tel: +(686) 28399
Sydney Office Tel: +(61) 29232551 Fax: +(61) 9232 5499
Email: info@kiribatiholidays.com
Website: http://www.kiribatiholidays.com

Islands

Kiritimati Island

The name "Kiritimati" is a rather straightforward respelling of the English word "Christmas" in the Kiribati language, in which the combination ti is pronounced s, and the name is thus pronounced /kəˈrɪsməs/. Although most non-Kiribati people still correctly say the island's name as Christmas or Christmas Island, the change in spelling sometimes results in those not "in the know" mispronouncing it as the letter combination "Kiritimati" would be pronounced in English.

The island has the greatest land area of any coral atoll in the world, about 388 square kilometres (150 square miles); its lagoon is roughly the same size. The atoll is about 150 km (93 mi) in perimeter, while the lagoon shoreline extends for over 48 km (30 mi). Kiritimati comprises over 70% of the total land area of Kiribati, a country encompassing 33 Pacific atolls and islands.

It lies 232 km (144 mi) north of the Equator, 2,160 km (1,340 mi) south of Honolulu, and 5,360 km (3,330 mi) from San Francisco. Kiritimati Island is in the world's farthest forward time zone, UTC+14, and is one of the first inhabited places on Earth to experience the New Year (see also Caroline Atoll, Kiribati). Despite being 2,460 km (1,530 mi) east of the 180 meridian, a 1995 realignment of the International Date Line by the Republic of Kiribati moved Kiritimati to west of the dateline.

Nuclear tests were conducted on and around Kiribati by the United Kingdom in the late 1950s, and by the United States in 1962. During these tests islanders were not evacuated. Subsequently, British, New Zealand, and Fijian servicemen as well as local islanders have claimed to have suffered from exposure to the radiation from these blasts.

The entire island is a Wildlife Sanctuary; access to five particularly sensitive areas (see below) is restricted.

Tabiteuea Island

Tabiteuea, formerly Drummond's Island, is an atoll in the Gilbert Islands, Kiribati, farther south of the Tarawa Atoll. The atoll consists of two main islands: Eanikai in the north, Nuguti in the south, and several smaller islets in between along the eastern rim of the atoll. The atoll has a total land area of 38 km2 (15 sq mi), while the lagoon measures 365 km2 (141 sq mi). The population numbered 4,899 in 2005.

While most atolls of the Gilbert Islands correspond to local government areas governed by island councils, Tabiteuea, like the main atoll Tarawa, is divided into two:

- ➢ Tabiteuea North has a land area of 26 km2 (10 sq mi) and a population of 3,600 as of 2005, distributed among twelve villages (capital Utiroa).
- ➢ Tabiteuea South has a land area of 12 km2 (4.6 sq mi) and a population of 1,299, distributed among six villages (capital Buariki).

"Tabiteuea" is Gilbertese for "land of no chiefs"; the island is traditionally egalitarian. In the late 1800s, the two islands were the site of a religious war when the populace of Tabiteuea North converted to Christianity and, led by a man called Kapu who had assembled a "hymn-singing army on a crusade", invaded and conquered Tabiteuea South, which had maintained traditional religious practice.

The Battle of Drummond's Island occurred during the United States Exploring Expedition in April 1841 at Tabiteuea, then known as Drummond's Island. After one sailor from sloop USS Peacock, was captured by the islanders, the US party decided on exacting redress for the incident. Twelve islanders were killed in the fighting and others were wounded.

During the US Civil War, the Confederate States Navy steamer CSS Shenandoah visited the island on March 23, 1865 in search of United States whalers, but the whalers had fled the area. Captain James Waddell described the islanders as "of copper colour, short of statue, athletic in form, intelligent and docile" and were "without a stitch of clothing".

Tabiteuea Post Office opened around 1911 and was renamed Tabiteuea North around 1972. Tabiteuea South Post Office opened on 13 September 1965.

Tarawa Island

Tarawa is an atoll and the capital of the Republic of Kiribati, in the central Pacific Ocean. It comprises North Tarawa, which has much in common with other, more remote islands of the Gilberts group; and South Tarawa, which is home to 50,182 as of 2010 – half of the country's total population. The atoll is best known by outsiders as the site of the Battle of Tarawa during World War II.

Tarawa has a large lagoon, 500 square kilometres (193 sq mi) total area, and a wide reef. Although naturally abundant in fish and shellfish of all kinds, marine resources are being strained by the large and growing population. Drought is frequent, but in normal years rainfall is sufficient to maintain breadfruit, papaya and banana trees as well as coconut and pandanus.

North Tarawa consists of a string of islets, with the most northern islet being Buariki. The islets are separated in places by wide channels that are best crossed at low tide.

On South Tarawa, the construction of causeways has now created a single strip of land from Betio in the West to Buota in the Northeast.

In Kiribati mythology, Tarawa was the earth when the land, ocean and sky had not been cleaved yet by Nareau the spider. Thus after calling the sky 'karawa' and the ocean 'marawa', he called the piece of rock that 'Riiki' (another god that Nareau found) had stood upon when he lifted up the sky as, 'Tarawa'. Nareau then created the rest of the islands in Kiribati and also Samoa.

People arrived on these islands thousands of years ago, and there have been migrations to and from Kiribati since antiquity.

Evidence from a range of sources, including carbon dating and DNA analyses, confirms that the exploration of the Pacific included settlement of the Gilbert Islands by around 200 BC. The people of Kiribati are still excellent seafarers, capable of making ocean crossings in locally-made vessels using traditional navigation techniques.

Thomas Gilbert, captain of the East India Company vessel Charlotte, was the first European to describe Tarawa, arriving on 20 June 1788. He named it Matthew Island, after the owner of his ship, the Charlotte. He named the lagoon, Charlotte Bay. Gilbert's 1788 sketches survive.

Tarawa Post Office opened on 1 January 1911.

Sir Arthur Grimble was a cadet administrative officer based at Tarawa (1913–1919); and became Resident Commissioner of the Gilbert and Ellice Islands colony in 1926.

During World War II, Tarawa was occupied by the Japanese, and beginning on 20 November 1943 it was the scene of the bloody Battle of Tarawa. On that day United States Marines landed on

Tarawa and suffered heavy losses from Japanese soldiers occupying entrenched positions on the atoll. The Marines secured the island after 76 hours of intense fighting with around 6,000 dead in total from both sides.

The Kiribati Government commenced a road restoration project funded in part by the World Bank in 2014 to surface the main road between Betio in the West to Bonriki in the East, upgrading the main road that transits Tarawa from a dirt road.

Airports

Bonriki International Airport

Situated to the northeast of the main town of Tarawa Atoll on the Gilbert Islands is Bonriki International Airport, the main gateway to Kiribati. Despite being the main hub, it is very basic with an open runway and limited facilities. Most flights arrive via Nadi in Fiji on Air Pacific or Air Kiribati twice weekly (Monday and Thursday), which takes three hours. You can also get in from Brisbane, Australia with Our Airline, as well as from the Solomon Islands and Fiji. Air Kiribati serves various destinations within the Gilbert Islands, as does the recently added Coral Sun Airways. It's only 10 minutes to Bonriki town by minibus, 20 to Bairiki and about 30 to Betio.

Cassidy International Airport

Unfortunately there are no domestic flights to Christmas Island, with access to Cassidy International Airport from Honolulu (Hawaii) and Nadi (Fiji) only on Air Pacific. Cassidy has a sealed runway, but its single terminal also has limited facilities. Banana village is a short trip from the airport, while London, the main town, is about 20 minutes by taxi.

Kanton Island Airport

Getting to the Phoenix Islands is by way of private, chartered aircraft from American Samoa, though you can only fly to Kanton Island. Reaching the Phoenix Island Marine Protected Area can be done by boat charter. As with the other smaller islands, Kanton Island Airport has very limited facilities.

Travel Tips

Language

English is Kiribati's official language, but most natives also speak the local Gilbertese tongue. You shouldn't have a problem communicating wherever you go, although the farther you get from Tarawa and Christmas Island, the less English is used.

Currency

Kiribati and the Islands use the Australian dollar; a major currency that can be exchanged anywhere. You can also change money at the Bank of Kiribati or ANZ bank on Tarawa or Christmas Island. Kiribati is a mostly cash-oriented country, though major cards are accepted in hotels and some shops. Traveler's checks should be in Aussie dollars.

Time

Kiribati is GMT+14 and the Line Islands are the first to see the new day.

Electricity

The power supply in Kiribati is 240V/50Hz, the same as in the UK. Plugs are of the I type with slotted three pins, the same as Australia. US travelers should have a converter and adapter if bringing electrical devices such as shavers and hairdryers. The latest smartphones (including iPhones) and laptops will often charge on either voltage.

Communications

Kiribati's country code +686. When dialing out, you usually have to go through the operator, and via radio telephone in the more remote islands. Mobile phones run on the GSM 900 network through Telecom Services Kiribati, though coverage is sketchy outside the capital. Internet connectivity is limited, with the odd internet café in towns and main hotels.

Duty-free

Duty-free allowances include up to 200 cigarettes or 225 g of cigars or tobacco, one liter of spirits and one liter of wine (if 21 years or older) and reasonable amounts of perfume and sports equipment. You can only bring in one camera and one pair of binoculars tax-free.

Tourist Office

Kiribati National Tourism Office, Tarawa: +686 25 573 or http://www.kiribatitourism.gov.ki

Emergency services: 999

Visas and Vaccinations

Visitors from North America, the UK (and rest of the EU), Australia, and New Zealand do not need a visa for stays in Kiribati up to 30 days. A valid passport and return/onward ticket are also mandatory, and you may be asked to provide evidence of funds for your stay. Vaccinations for diphtheria and hepatitis A are recommended.

Health and Safety

Kiribati is one of the safer places in the world; certainly more so than Hawaii in the sense of crime. Busier areas, however, do have some problems, though mostly petty crime such as pick pocketing in the towns. It is best to avoid Beito and South Tarawa beaches after sundown and single females should exercise special caution by night.

While dengue fever can break out on occasion (no vaccine for this), Kiribati is malaria-free so no need for anti-malarials. Visitors should always have a quality insect repellant to hand, though, and use liberally at night.

There is just the one hospital in Kiribati, the Tungaru Central, which is located in South Tarawa. It is a basic facility and visitors will have to pay for treatment, so keep receipts for any visits. The hospital sends medicines out to dispensaries for the other atolls, which are also basic. Bring a supply of any medicines you might be on and note their generic name.

Lagoon swimming is safest, although Tarawa Lagoon should be avoided near the towns due to the pollution. Be careful when swimming or snorkeling on ocean-facing reefs. It is best to go with a tour when visiting remoter places if you intend on snorkeling or, at the least, check with locals on conditions. Tarawa roads can be tough due to cattle traffic and the free-for-all driving manner of local drivers.

Holidays and Festivals

Kiribati holidays include an intriguing line-up of events, from the first to celebrate the New Year to a lively independence day "week" and a boisterous Christmas period. Traditional singing and dancing can be enjoyed at all times.

New Year's Day

Kiribati is the first country in the world to welcome in the New Year, albeit at the Line Islands, and events go off nationwide. All bars and guesthouses have something going on, along with traditional celebrations at the local *maneaba* (meeting house).

Independence Day

This is the main event on the Kiribati social calendar, celebrating the day the Gilbert Islands gained independence from Great Britain in July of 1979. Though the holiday officially takes place on July 12, the festivities last for several days, starting around the 9th. South Tarawa sees most of the action, including obligatory canoe races, kite-flying and traditional dance, along with wrestling, rugby and other sports ventures.

Youth Day

August 4 sees the forward-thinking government focus its energy on the Kiribati youth, with the promise of better opportunities through various workshops and programs. Churches and meeting houses see most activity.

Christmas

Locals attend church followed by much eating, gift-giving and merriment, just like they do back home. In Kiribati, however, there's also choir singing, dancing, canoe racing, and a myriad of other sports right up until New Year. Locals also go camping in Taiwan Park and visit nearby islands.

New Year's Eve

A huge event in Kiribati due to its position in the world, this island nation is the first place to countdown the New Year. There are low-key parties on the beaches and in the towns, while all expat bars and guesthouses put on special events.

Betio Game Fishing Competition

This is a popular event among expats in South Tarawa, with a monthly competition and weight-ins at Captains Bar in Betio to see the biggest catches.

Kiribati Music and Dance

Kiribati folk music and dance is unique to the region, with chanting accompanied by body percussion and guitar, while dance is typically bird-like with costumed performers. *Maneaba* have music and dance nightly in-season.

Weather

Kiribati's weather is hot, humid, rainy, and fairly predictable. This is partially due to the country's location nearly on the equator, which tends to temper weather extremes from both a temperature and a rain standpoint. This steady climate of rain and humidity help make the islands livable as fresh water is regularly available through rain. However, as a primarily coralline island nation, the soils still aren't excellent, so the rains do little more than allow human survival on the islands

The temperatures on the islands remain quite stable year round as daily lows hover around 72° F (22° C) and day time highs usually peak at about 79° F (26° C). With this heat is a regular humidity as well as fairly constant rains.

The northern Line Islands in the east get the most rain with an average of about 2 feet (600 mm) per month, although Christmas

Island, also in this island chain, gets much less. These rains are fairly regular throughout the year, but tend to be a bit higher in the months of November to May, also known as the wet season in Kiribati. The Gilbert Islands in the far western part of the country get much less rain with an average of about 10 inches (250 mm) per month, and again the months of November to May tend to have a bit more than that average, while the rest of the months tend to get a bit less than that average.

Although cyclones are well known throughout the Pacific, Kiribati falls out of the cyclone zone. Despite this, heavy storms and cyclones can still hit the islands any time of year, but are most common from November to May.

www.ingramcontent.com/pod-product-compliance
Lightning Source LLC
Chambersburg PA
CBHW021112080526
44587CB00010B/491